PROPERTY DEVELOPMENT

EXPLAINED SIMPLY

STEVE PALISE & LIAM CARMODY

MAJOR STREET

MAJOR STREET

First published in 2025 by Major Street Publishing Pty Ltd
info@majorstreet.com.au | majorstreet.com.au

A catalogue record for this book is available
from the National Library of Australia

NATIONAL LIBRARY OF AUSTRALIA

Printed book ISBN: 978-1-923186-25-5
Ebook ISBN: 978-1-923186-26-2

Cover design by Tess McCabe
Internal design by Production Works

10 9 8 7 6 5 4 3 2 1

CONTENTS

WHY PROPERTY DEVELOPMENT?

You may have read the first book in this series, *Commercial Property Investing Explained Simply*, and the follow-up book, *Residential Property Investing Explained Simply*. After Steve wrote both, we've helped thousands of new and seasoned people find their footing or elevate their learning by investing in property.

But there's a third piece in the property toolkit: development. It's the missing link, the last piece of the puzzle to give you the FULL picture for successful property investment. So, we decided to make property development the focus of the third book in our series: planning, building and marketing to create profit levels that eclipse BOTH residential and commercial investing!

Steve's story

You probably already know me from my other two books, so I will keep it brief here.

In 2012, I chose property as my path to financial independence. From buying my very first residential house in Blacktown (in western Sydney, New South Wales) to ditching my engineering career and launching full-time into property, I knew I was on the money when I made this my life's work.

I learnt a lot from those days of buying, selling, profiting and refinancing. I made some property development mistakes – a couple costly – but I knew I'd never go back to working nine to five, nor leave my financial future in the hands of a faceless corporate machine.

Instead, I grew a life better aligned with my goals – travelling, socialising, climbing mountains, feeling appreciated and working on passion projects. One of my achievements was travelling to 35 countries by the time I turned 35 without sacrificing my professional career or my relationships.

In 2021, I relocated to England with my wife for two years. During that time, we were based in Brighton, and I worked in 15 countries, also boosting my countries visited to 50. Despite my business being back home in Sydney, I was able to manage all work and travel through my mixture of property investments, including residential, commercial – and development.

While in the UK, I had a chance encounter with another Australian, Liam Carmody. Like me, Liam has an engineering background and obsesses over data and numbers. Coincidentally, we both have British wives, and my partner said his personality is almost identical to mine. (Hopefully she thinks I am better looking, though!) He's perfect for property and even better for a career in property development. We instantly clicked through our disillusion with our former engineering careers and our shared philosophy of property as a vehicle for wealth.

Years later, here we are! Liam has been part of the Palise Property family since near inception, and our values haven't changed – they're about spending time with our families and sharing our knowledge to help others on their own wealth journeys. Property can give you the life you desire, and this is why I love it.

When it came to the third book in this series, I wanted the right person to help tell the story, and that's why you see two authors on the cover instead of one. Liam is the perfect person for the job. After all, two heads are better than one, right?

Liam's story

I grew up in a small country town southwest of Sydney called Yass. Even from an early age, I was paving the way for a career in property.

In a household of brothers (I am the eldest of three), my home environment was very competitive. With sport, it was always about who was the fastest swimmer, who had the lowest golf handicap, or who scored the most tries in rugby or the most runs in cricket. The only way to achieve these things was through practice, repetition and dedication. When it came to schoolwork, it was no different!

Then, when I was going into Year 10, my parents made the big financial decision to send my brothers and me to a large private school in Canberra. To get there each day, we had to wake up at 5.30 a.m. to ride the bus for an hour and a half each way. If we missed the bus, we would need to be driven to school, so there was an incentive not to be late to avoid the wrath of our parents! Those early starts have stuck with me ever since. I can see they were the foundations of my work ethic, and I have my parents to thank for that.

At around the same time, I got my first taste of property development. For my Year 10 work experience program, I spent three weeks shadowing one of our family friends, an established and still practising property developer in Canberra. He placed me in different consultants' offices, from architects to town planners to engineers, which gave me an understanding of this space from a variety of angles.

I particularly loved the building and problem-solving aspect that engineering offered. Thinking this was the best mix for me to start a career in property development, I went on to study civil engineering at the University of Wollongong, obtaining an honours degree.

Six months before graduating, I got a job in a tier-one civil construction company on a $300 million road project. But my heart wasn't in it. I was earning good money working with great people, but at the end of the day, I was never passionate about building roads. My interest was always in property. For the time being, though, I grew my engineering knowledge and used the job to help fund my property endeavours.

The light-bulb moment came when my mum was in a cancer treatment ward over a decade ago. On the first occasion I took Mum for her treatment, I needed a distraction from what was happening around me. When my eye caught the cover of the *Australian Property Investor* magazine sitting on a table, I picked it up hungrily.

I was hooked! I inhaled every investor story word for word, fascinated by their journeys and how investing could provide financial freedom. Each article was accompanied by data and tables, and by looking at these closely I could see that the answers were staring back at me in black and white. I knew this was where I needed to focus my attention. Of course, with my mum in hospital, the timing was pivotal as I could truly see how quickly life can change.

Every month I bought the magazine and read it front to back to understand all the different strategies. Then, I made my own spreadsheets of research tracking market trends, which eventually helped me get into the property market purchasing my first property in Wollongong.

Within 12 months, I had built up enough equity to buy my first investment property, and then I continued this process, purchasing property every year through recycling equity. Eventually, I was making more than six figures annually by growing my property portfolio. By combining property investment and engineering, I found my true passion – property development.

What surprises me with property development is how many potential sites don't stack up. Property 'experts' will tout the next hot spot, but the key is education and understanding the market you're looking in. You have to be the area expert, which will not only protect you from risks but also open up off-market opportunities.

This is how I secured my first site, and having that local knowledge allowed me to make a quick decision. Having great contacts with local town planners, architects and builders who you can rely on for expertise and advice is a huge help when assessing development opportunities. I've also found it hugely beneficial and inspiring to have mentors who are experienced and trustworthy.

Today, I have several developments and properties around Australia as well as a side business, Continual Development, which operates mutually alongside Palise Property. As the name suggests, the company is about continually evolving and developing. Every project is different, and the purpose for doing it needs to be clearly defined from the start.

To me, property development is the ultimate active strategy. It's not for the faint-hearted, and there are always obstacles and hurdles along the way, but the rewards are beyond what you can achieve through any other form of investing. It's hugely satisfying to create income for ourselves and others while giving the market properties we can be proud of. With a clear direction and goal, you'll continue to move forward – and hopefully strive to achieve your goals and aspirations. My ultimate goal is to continue to develop and have more of what means the most to me personally – time and family.

After taking some time off from engineering to spend time with my young family during COVID-19, I had a chance meeting with Steve Palise in the UK. He had recently started his own business and was looking for someone like-minded to assist him. Fast-forward a handful of years and here we are!

Bringing it together

We've written the third and final book in this series to give you the FULL picture of property investment. Many authors try and direct you to their core business for financial gain – our approach is to give you ALL the options so you can decide for yourself. After all, there's very little on bookshop shelves about property development, and it can be hard to understand the full process and activity.

Property development is an incredibly powerful tool that can accelerate your property goals drastically. From duplex developments to apartment complexes and commercial retail developments, the sector covers many properties where land or buildings are converted into profitable real estate projects. From acquiring the land or property to feasibility, securing financing, design and construction, and then finally marketing and sales, the development process comprises the full gamut of bringing a project to life – and then navigating the legal, financial and market challenges along the way to ensure its long-term success and profitability.

The benefits are hugely attractive. Developers make money by increasing their property's value as well as through the rental income it generates year on year. In other words, by forcing value on an asset (without waiting for capital growth or relying on cash flow), you can reach your target for portfolio size, passive income or retirement much sooner.

Property development is a space feared by most and trialled by few. Those who spruik it talk about cutting deals together, making millions, parading around in fast cars and smooth clothes and drinking lattes all day, but the truth is that, of the hundreds of investors who want that life, only very few do it successfully. We both say that property development is not for the faint-hearted. It requires confidence, risk, education and knowledge – and the most successful developers often try a few other investment types first.

In this third book, we give you the complete picture of how to make money in developing real estate. We show you that with the right education and the combined knowledge of two authors with decades of property experience and thousands of acquisitions under their belts, you can make an informed decision about what's right for you and your future.

Let's go on a journey and explore the world of property development. The style and insights of this book follow a similar format to the first two books, in the hope that it's easy to follow, understand and, hopefully, implement. You'll read horror stories from experts who have seen it all, and there are real-life case studies to learn from as well. Plus, you'll meet our Big Figures (BIGFIGs), you'll learn more about these later. From start to finish, we'll show you the best and right ways to develop real estate, coming from two investors leading the industry.

By presenting all the options, you'll be better informed to choose the right solution and plan for you – whatever that looks like. With education comes knowledge, and with insight comes better risk mitigation – and, ultimately, success.

Are you ready?

PART I
WHAT IS PROPERTY DEVELOPMENT?

The Cambridge Dictionary definition of property development is, *'the process of buying, improving, and selling buildings and land, and arranging for new buildings to be built'*. In other words, it's about 'improving' a piece of land's usable capabilities. It's an advanced form of property investment, over and above simply buying and selling, offering financial rewards that can be highly lucrative, as well as providing a wealth creation vehicle that can set you up for life. It's addictive and a brilliant way to create something tangible not only for yourself but your community for the future. That's why we feel so strongly about it as an investment class!

Property development is also complex and challenging. You need a solid understanding of the market drivers, construction know-how and cost management skills, and a strategy that works for anyone from seasoned investors to mum-and-dad developers.

Because of its versatility and varying levels of complexity, it appeals to a range of investors. A development could be anything from turning one house into two duplexes (even considering the development potential of the family home to knock down and subdivide) to turning a vacant block into a 500-unit apartment tower. Furthermore, renovations can also be seen as 'developments', although most established developers actively attempt to change the asset type to revalue it at a profit that would be worth the risk and time involved to do so.

If you remember that property development is about how the land is used to enhance its value, you can start to think more broadly. For example, successful property development doesn't have to be confined to the residential sector. In fact, there are many scenarios where the property's use case is changed to improve the land's capabilities – think abandoned warehouses in inner-city Melbourne rezoned and transformed into boutique townhouses.

The upsides of property development

The key benefit of property development is being able to turn a profit in several different ways: by keeping the development, holding it or selling it, depending on the strategy. Let's look at a few ways you can turn an excellent profit.

Doing a development is one of the fastest ways to achieve your property goals – whether you have a net wealth target, a passive income target or both! Because you can force value upon a property, you can reach your goals more quickly.

Choosing to hold a development – that is, you don't sell for profit – can provide a passive income faster than traditional buy-and-hold strategies. For example, a project with a 20 per cent profit margin means the value of your portfolio will be 20 per cent greater – instantly.

Furthermore, if you keep your own stock as opposed to buying someone else's end product, you're getting the property at raw cost (saving on acquisition costs such as stamp duty and legal fees), so you're effectively getting it wholesale (typically 15 to 30 per cent cheaper than what the market would pay)! This will give you a better loan-to-value ratio (LVR) position and a higher yield than buying property at the market rate, meaning you'll have more cash flow and better servicing when looking to buy future properties. As we mentioned earlier, if you keep your own stock, you have manufactured capital growth; this means you'll have more equity in the build than what you can buy at market rate.

Another key benefit is the ability to use creative strategies and development finance to grow your portfolio. Investors love the idea of being able to control everything about the design, construction and marketing of the development to differentiate it from everything else on the market.

Some of the more advanced strategies are later in the book. For example, another benefit is the ability to leverage commercial finance to get a higher return on investment (ROI) and cash-on-cash (COC) return. This can work brilliantly in markets with high demand for new properties. It's also common practice for developers to have 'money partners', meaning you can manage the project and leverage someone else's money – you don't have to use your own cash.

You can take advantage of government incentives and subsidies, which are available across Australia. For example, the HomeBuilder program provides cash grants to use to build a new home, renovate an existing home or buy off the plan, subject to eligibility.

There are great benefits that come with new builds. For example, it can be easier to attract tenants because they like new, shiny things, and the property can be easier to maintain with its sparkling fittings and fixtures. You can also make the most of depreciation benefits for newly constructed homes; you can read about what you can claim and when in Steve's previous two books.

Downsizers make up a huge portion of the market; they are seeking to trade out of their older properties that are becoming too much of a burden to maintain. Smaller and newer properties such as townhouses, duplexes or apartments with good accessibility and low maintenance are in high demand with this demographic. A flow-on effect from this shift is increased demand for storage facilities or small industrial properties, because these downsizers still require places to put their belongings or 'toys'.

The downsides of property development

You probably don't need us to tell you that property development is complicated and risky! It's not for the uneducated, and it requires experience to excel. Most people will have already enjoyed some level of success with other property types before tackling a development, but don't forget that everyone has to start somewhere. Don't be intimidated by others' stories. There's no shortage of fresh investors ready to take the plunge with the right level of well-educated guidance (starting here, of course).

Funding can be difficult to lock in, meaning that it typically helps to be established. There are creative funding methods out there, though, with higher risk. We cover this later in the book, but here is a summary of some of these methods:

- **Cash.** Cash or personal funds is the best way to finance property development. It can keep costs down and also avoid interest charges.

- **Equity.** Refinancing from existing properties or investments to help fund a project can be a great way to increase your net wealth. In addition, the interest charged on the equity you use is tax-deductible.

- **Property development loans.** These are specialised loans that give you funds for the total development cost, repaid at the end of the construction period as you sell off the project.

- **Equity partners.** An equity partner is someone who provides equity for a development and in return will receive a profit share. In most cases, you as the developer will remain in control of the overall development, and the equity partner will benefit from your knowledge and time. The equity partner will be on the title and loan, sharing this risk and responsibility with you, the developer.

- **Money partners.** A money partner gives you the capital you need, while you provide the development strategy and knowledge. A money partner is different from an equity partner in that they will receive an interest-rate return on their money for the period of time they're invested in the development. The security will most likely be in the form of a second mortgage. A good partnership can be hugely beneficial, especially when you've built up trust in the relationship. Great sources of money partners can be through private finance; your own network of accountants, solicitors or business owners; and self-managed superannuation funds (SMSFs). Note that you can't use your own SMSF to fund your own projects.

Financing a development isn't as easy as finding a broker and working out your borrowing capacity. You need a whole team (more on that later) and skill to manage each one in the right order throughout your development. The balancing act required to manage each of the stakeholders in your team can be a full-time job!

With so many options, and with so much time and knowledge required to pull off a successful development, the work can be tedious and all-consuming. From local council regulations to unforeseen delays in finance approvals and unexpected costs, the amount of time needed to dedicate to developments is often underestimated.

Developments are also subject to market volatility. For example, if the costs of labour, steel, concrete or timber increase during the process, this can eat into your profit. Similarly, if the market you were hoping to sell in falls in value, you may not pocket as much as you expected. Longer-than-anticipated construction times can also have an effect. If you can imagine how much a market can change over one year, imagine if your development took three years from start to completion; the market you're selling in could be completely different to when you began the development.

Overview of property development in Australia

Essentially, people need homes. Whether it's a house, duplex, townhouse or apartment, everyone needs somewhere to live that provides accommodation, safety and comfort. In addition, people need services and infrastructure – think mechanics or fabricators, and warehouses to distribute goods. They also need in-person retail and health services such as medical centres, cafes and hairdressers. As a developer, your ability to bring infill supply into a suburb could deliver you significant profits, whether you keep or sell the property. And as property markets and demographics change over time, developers are incentivised to build what people want to live in – that's basic capitalism.

What is the current housing snapshot?

At time of writing, reports fill the newspaper pages every day about a housing affordability crisis that no quick bandaid can fix. Building approvals are at an all-time low, and despite increased demand, there are fewer buildings available in the aftermath of a year of rising interest rates, and inflation is at the highest levels in more than 30 years.

The rental market is also in crisis, which is exacerbated by the slowing rate of construction, a fall in new builds, subdued investor activity and the higher proportion of income required to pay for rent. Higher-than-forecast migration numbers (737,000 in 2022–23, up 73 per cent from the previous year) are also putting pressure on rental availability and prices, as well as adding to the surging cost of living many Australians are experiencing.

Medium- and high-density developments will become increasingly important in making housing more affordable and reducing the rental crisis. The 'Great Australian Dream' of a standalone house on a quarter-acre block that so many Australians aspired to is almost gone, and in its place are different paths to home ownership that embrace a mix of housing types.

As Australia accepts more immigrants, there will need to be more solutions to boost housing supply. Regulations may be eased to favour developers, such as smaller dwelling-size limits or fewer requirements around parking available on the site and street.

What are the opportunities?

At the time of writing, property development is losing its appeal to some people. High interest rates, increased building costs, lower-than-previous borrowing capacity and a risk-averse stance on developments that may take longer and result in increased holding costs all add up to excessive risk. While the last ten years were very kind to developers – most of Australia's largest cities experienced between 50 and 100 per cent capital growth with incredibly low interest rates – the game has now changed.

However, all we see are opportunities. If housing demand is critically high and supply critically low, we are in a position to solve a core problem by creating innovative solutions to boost supply. If the incentive is strong enough, a developer might just find some developable gems at less of a premium than previously thought.

Building wealth through property development is a great way to fast-track a passive income, especially compared to the 30-year approach of paying down your mortgage. Property development can typically offer between 15 and 30 per cent ROI to an investor, as well as a limitless COC return as you become more experienced. Imagine creating an extra $500,000 per year for yourself and your family to either live off or invest in other passive assets, such as commercial property.

Smaller projects that take six to eight months can increase your yearly return to more than 30 per cent. By doing them, you can build equity for yourself, and in some cases they may be fully paid off at completion.

Let's look at a basic example from an investor's perspective, ignoring taxes, purchasing costs and selling costs to keep it simple. As a money partner, say you inject $1 million cash into a prop-erty development that gives you a 20 per cent return, making you $200,000 over and above your initial investment. If you then put that $1.2 million of capital into the next property development and it gives you the same rate of return, you would be left with $1.44 million. After five such developments, your initial $1 million could transform into $2.48 million, and after ten developments it could be $6.19 million. This is the effect of compounding returns.

As another example, if you invest in a project as an equity partner, you can take advantage of one of the other important elements of property development: leverage. You can share in the total profits, which can mean your COC return can be 50 per cent or more! If you leverage these profits into another larger development, then you can potentially earn five times more and compound the above returns again.

Let's keep going. Building further on the previous examples, you could also adopt a strategy of 'build six, keep one' or 'build 12, keep two', because holding properties will bring you further wealth through capital growth. In most cases, the profit in a project comes from the last sales – once you have paid out the lenders, investors and builder, and recovered other costs involved in the project. Instead of taking this profit out, you might decide to keep some of the residual stock. This can leave you holding an asset with minimal or no debt, built at raw cost, that is also providing you passive income. Talk about a win-win!

Please note that this is illustrative – there are many more ins and outs involved, which we will cover in this book.

Once you have some experience and gain a reputation for developing, you may be able to use capital partners to manage multiple projects without using your own equity, as touched on earlier.

This is the great thing about property development – it gives you so many brilliant options that traditional residential or commercial investing do not.

Public and social need

Developers built the communities you live in today. Do you think the government built that newly renovated local shopping village? No. It was a developer, who was incentivised by profit and fortunately worked out that it was viable to do so. As a result, the community benefits. Similarly, developers are responsible for the house-and-land packages that allow communities to expand, turning previously empty fields into new estates and giving young families an affordable place to live. Developers sometimes get a bad rap for apartment towers in particular, but there are just as many great developers producing quality products.

Given there are about 50,000 people waiting for affordable housing and government housing incentives at the time of writing, the demand – and the opportunity for developers – is there. Governments already incentivise developers with concessions to build National Rental and Affordability Scheme (NRAS) and National Disability and Insurance Scheme (NDIS) developments, for example, while the planning code allows developers who allocate a certain portion of an investment to affordable housing or who secure a Complying Development Certificate (CDC) to build higher than the maximum zoning or increase the density to maximise the floor space. Governments are pushing for a proportion of new developments to be dedicated to public housing, but no new development is typically viable without these concessions.

As we mentioned earlier, as immigration increases and Australia's population grows, it's becoming harder to meet housing needs. Building approvals are at an all-time low and councils are scrutinising developers harder than ever. As a result, approximately 650,000 people in Australia are living in distress due to the housing crisis, and it is estimated that it will take 10 to 20 years to overcome the current challenge.

Over the next five years, it's predicted that Australia will require another 1.2 million homes to keep up with demand due to the increase in population. Based on current forecasts, we are likely to fall 250,000 homes short of this number. Put simply, more homes need to be built to increase the supply and soothe the current housing crisis.

A shift in attitude needs to be made to support development and property developers. For the most part, property development is an extremely risky and difficult business, dealing with banks, financing, councils, red tape, construction and regulation. We'd love to see the public, councils and the government get behind developers so that we can all create some positive outcomes for the housing industry and our communities.

Setting your goals

Maybe it's because people like round numbers, or maybe it just sounds impressive, but for many people a common first goal is either to achieve $100,000 in passive income per year or have a $5 million portfolio. Whenever our clients say they want to achieve a particular number, we cheekily respond, 'And then what?'

We need to delve a little deeper into why that is their goal, and that'll reveal the real driver behind wealth creation. Some do not even know their 'why' – they're just on the hamster wheel of thinking that wealth will bring happiness. The answer is usually to be able to upgrade the family home, spend more time with children, travel or quit a job and work on a passion project, or a combination of these.

After writing two books and several courses, programs and media, we've met and spoken with thousands of people from different walks of life. We love meeting a big mix – anyone from ultra-high-net-worth clients to low-income earners, and the funny thing is that you never know what's going on behind closed doors. Some clients you'd expect to be happy are miserable, and vice versa.

Everyone's version of happiness is different, so the key is to block out the noise and work out what your version is – without the barrage of information on how to do this.

While property development is not all smooth sailing and is stressful at times, it's rewarding, especially when your goals are meaningful and genuine.

There are also myths around property development, but these are just misunderstandings. The reality is that it's like climbing a staircase: if you were to just buy a house to live in, this would be your first step, and if you were to buy an investment property, that would require a few more steps (as you would need to understand market fundamentals and growth factors). Property development has these steps plus many more! It's not that each step is difficult, it's just that there are a lot of them to master – or, if you're not educated, more to fall down!

Most people, however, overestimate what they need to achieve their happiness goals, and this means taking unnecessary risks. So, before you consider whether property development is right for you, it's important to decide what goals will make you happy. What motivates you?

What are your short-, medium- and long-term goals?

Property investing has enabled the two of us to pursue our goals – travelling, spending more time with our families and working when we want to.

Everyone is different. For instance, Liam loves the thrill of property development and solving problems, which brings him joy; Steve loves the outcome of what property brings him but does not enjoy the process as much. Liam's focus is on building net wealth; Steve's focus is on building passive income. Property development can suit both of our strategies.

Be realistic with your goals and don't just come up with a random portfolio size or passive-income amount. Sacrificing time today for a specific number tomorrow may not be consistent with your personal values. It can also mean you take on unnecessary risk that does not provide your life with any more joy.

Think about these questions:

- What are you trying to achieve from undertaking a property development?
- Why are you trying to achieve this goal?

- What timeframe do you want to reach your goals in?
- Why is this important to you?
- What is your risk profile, and does property development suit it?

Steve and Liam's tips

Property development can achieve your goals – whatever they may be – faster than any other property method. Let this be a motivator for you too!

What type of developer do you want to be?

Every property investor has unique characteristics – there is no one-size-fits-all property investment strategy or type. When expanding your property portfolio with development, it's crucial to identify your objectives and feasibility to discern the appropriate strategy and investment types for you. Understanding your risk profile is key to aligning your property development strategy with your goals and anticipating outcomes accurately.

For example, some developers are know-it-alls, while others rely on tradie mates to help out for a good price. Some think it runs in the family because a relative was a developer, while others try to band together with family members to protect a generational asset instead of selling it. Everyone's starting point is different, and how you get to your end goal can also vary dramatically. Just like a road trip, the key is to decide where you want to go and plan how you can get there as safely as possible.

Think about these questions:

- Are you more of a risk taker or a conservative type of person?
- How active do you want to be in the project?
- How much time do you have available to you?

What's your risk profile?

Consider how your financial and life circumstances influence your risk tolerance and investment goals. You need to look at the stability of your income. This will come down to what career you have; for example a nurse typically has a lower chance of losing their job than someone in a commission-based role or in a volatile industry. You then need to cross-check this with your liabilities (that is, current loans, expenses and dependants, such as kids).

Balance your desired returns with your risk tolerance when selecting properties. Assess your reaction to market fluctuations and potential losses. Determine whether you prioritise a steady income or long-term growth, and adjust your strategy accordingly.

Where do you see yourself:

- **Conservative** – prefer low-volatility assets for steady positive returns
- **Balanced** – moderate risk tolerance, balancing growth and income assets
- **Aggressive** – embrace high-growth strategies like property development, accepting higher risks for potential returns.

What's your budget?

What do you need to have (a dollar-amount baseline) in order to undertake a property development? What's the 'easiest' development you can do with the least amount of dollars? What's a good budget to have?

These are all valid questions to ask, and you need to be sure that your budget is aligned with your goals. You might find your goals do not require you to use your full borrowing capacity, so why take on the extra risk?

Evaluate your financial stability to determine your capacity for risk, and compare a stable income versus volatile cash flows to gauge risk tolerance.

Remember that your debt levels and financial obligations will influence your risk capacity and borrowing power.

How much spare time do you have?

Property development can be a full-time job! You need to be clear on whether this is just a short-term project, a 'side business', or whether you want to step out of your current nine-to-five job and become a developer full time. If you're still working in a full-time job, you need to figure out how you'll manage the time required to successfully complete a project. This could mean getting up early before the kids wake up, or staying up late, or talking with your employer about flexible working arrangements.

Steve and Liam's tips

Having a supportive partner or network as you navigate the time requirements can be crucial. They will help you through the good times and the more challenging times (though hopefully you'll avoid those). How you navigate this comes back to your goals and timeframe.

What structure should you use?

At the earliest stage of a development, it makes sense to understand what type of development structure you'll embark upon. This might mean going solo or forming a partnership or a joint venture – there are many types of structures. You'll also need to work out how much to borrow from traditional lenders and whether you'll have access to investors or private finance. We cover all of this in Part IV.

Also, it's a good idea to have a handle on your exit strategies, even from the start. What are your plans for after completion – hold the entire property, refinance and keep, partly sell the development or completely sell the whole thing?

All of this and more is covered within these pages.

PART II
TYPES OF PROPERTY DEVELOPMENT

A chat around the barbecue or water cooler on anything to do with property development will reveal varying levels of understanding and experience. While there are plenty of options, from land subdivision to duplex development or, for more advanced investors, a larger residential or commercial development, you can be sure of one thing: if it's on land, it's an opportunity. The challenge lies in what to do with it, where it is and how you can get the best outcome for not only your pocket but also the local community. As Steve explored in his previous books, success in investing is purely a numbers game, and you need to be careful not to get swept up in the aesthetics and emotions of a property. Instead, understand how the right type of property will yield investing success for your growing portfolio. With this in mind, let's look at the most common types of property developments that you should consider investing in, and the pros and cons of holding or selling. You may already be familiar with them, but this time we'll look at them through a developer's lens. Let's go!

CHAPTER ONE
RESIDENTIAL

Residential property is the property class Australians know and love. To learn the fundamentals of residential investing, please see Steve's book *Residential Property Investing Explained Simply*. To develop residential property, read on.

Subdivision of land

The subdivision of land is the process of splitting a larger parcel of land into two or more parcels. Sometimes a lot that already has a house on it can be subdivided if there is room for another. Upon completion, the development will provide an increased number of lots, with new access and utilities to service each lot. The new lots will each have their own 'lot number' and attract rates and levies from council once registered.

The registering of the lots is a process whereby all the documents from the subdivision are submitted to council, including but not limited to survey plans, civil engineering plans, payment of council contributions by the developer and sign-off from certifiers.

The developer then has the option to either sell or hold the empty lots, or build and then sell or hold the completed lots.

Holding

Holding the subdivided lots is cash intensive, since the vacant parcels of land won't generate an income. For that reason, many developers who purchase land to hold will do so in cash. The benefit of holding the land is for capital growth through the increase in land prices. As a developer, the lots you want to hold onto are the best lots in the development. These will attract a higher price, especially after you have sold off all the other lots in the development and the demand remains high.

Typically, you would not adopt this strategy unless you were planning to extract equity or build a dwelling for cash flow.

Selling

Selling vacant lots of land is all about understanding supply and demand – being the local expert in your area and having intricate knowledge of how many potential buyers are looking to either move to the area, upgrade or purchase investment properties. Local builders are also a great resource as they may be looking to purchase vacant lots to build on and then sell themselves.

The timeframe for selling vacant land is much quicker than building and selling on completion. If the market is strong, it can be a lower-risk way to get in and out of the project quickly and achieve fantastic returns! As the developer, you'll need to understand what the highest and best use is (see chapter 5 for more on this), as the profit may not be higher if you were to build on vacant lots and sell on completion. Even if the profit is slightly lower, it may be the best option from a risk point of view, as it doesn't carry the same risk as building and being exposed to market changes.

Duplex

A duplex is in essence two properties side by side with an adjoining internal wall. These properties can exist on one land title and subsequently be sold or owned together, or they can be split onto separate titles and therefore be owned individually and sold.

There are also dual-income dwellings known as 'dual-key'. They look like a normal house and are similar to duplexes as they have two tenants, but they can't have separate titles. This is the same arrangement as a house with a granny flat, where you can't get a separate title for the granny flat; think of dual-keys as 'attached' granny flats.

Duplexes are becoming more and more prevalent in high-demand locations where land is at a premium. They enable people to buy in suburbs where they typically couldn't afford a freestanding house. The target market is often downsizers who don't want to move away from their current location and would prefer newer property and lower maintenance needs, or first home buyers who don't want to live in an apartment but don't have the ability to purchase a freestanding home.

Duplexes are becoming popular with residential investors as they can achieve higher cash flow returns than with standalone, single-tenant investments.

Holding

Holding a duplex can produce a high cash flow return due to the dual income streams and the corresponding yields you get for this type of asset. Having more than one income stream also mitigates risk. As there is no strata cost, the cash flow is higher than holding an apartment or townhouse, for example.

The other benefit is the option to sell one side of the duplex and hold the other one to reduce the level of debt and increase the rental yield. Remember, though, that the maintenance on the property in the long term will typically be higher, with two sets of kitchens, bathrooms, air conditioners, and so on.

Selling

As mentioned earlier, upon completion you have the option of selling one or both of the properties. When assessing the sales, it's important to consider if one side will be seen by potential buyers as premium or 'better' in general. This can come down to several factors, such as layout, views or the number of bedrooms, living spaces, car spaces, and so on. Selling the less attractive lot first can help to achieve the highest and best price for the remaining lot and attract a fear of missing out. It also means you don't allow buyers the choice between the two, which can risk bringing both sale prices down.

Townhouse

Townhouses are typically seen in the middle-ring regions of cities, where the zoning permits a higher density of housing. Most town-houses have common walls (although some are freestanding), shared parking, and shared amenities and services within the complex. Townhouses can be built over one, two or three levels (depending on council guidelines) and each has access to a private courtyard on the ground floor.

While attractive, access to shared facilities within a complex comes at a cost via strata or body corporate fees. These fees cover the general maintenance and upgrades of shared facilities in the complex, along with building insurance.

Townhouses cater to a wide range of users, from renters to investors, first home buyers, downsizers, young professionals and young families. The land component is smaller per townhouse than a standalone house, which opens more possibilities for people to enter the market at a lower entry point without having to sacrifice on location.

Holding

Similar to duplexes, developers have the option to hold onto residual stock at 'cost price' and achieve greater cash flow returns. Townhouses have higher holding costs when it comes to strata or body corporate fees (unless you hold the entire complex and self-manage it). Townhouse developments can range in size from three or four townhouses to dozens, so again, this can offer lower risk from a cash flow perspective as you're holding multiple assets with multiple income streams. For example, if you hold four tenanted townhouses and one tenant leaves, you still obtain 75 per cent of the original rental income.

Selling

Depending on the scale of the townhouse development, it's usually better to stage the sales. The sales can be done through a combination of 'off the plan' and 'sales upon completion' processes. When it comes to financing the project, particularly for larger sites, a financier will often require up to 50 per cent pre-sales to provide construction finance if there is inadequate capital from the developer.

Selling progressively over stages has several advantages and can help mitigate risk. It's important to track sales demand at each stage, as it can become apparent that if demand is low, it may be better to delay a subsequent stage of the project. By making too much stock available, you risk reducing the potential sale prices and therefore losing profit in the development. It's also important to keep track of nearby competing projects for the same reason.

Apartment complex

Apartment complexes are the widest-ranging residential property type in terms of scale. They can be as small as four-unit walk-up apartment blocks to multi-storey high-rise apartments with hundreds of units within a complex. Large-scale apartment complexes are often close to CBDs; however, due to the recent spike in housing unaffordability, they can be found in all regions of major cities. To obtain building approvals, they're usually required to be near infrastructure such as train stations and airports, and amenities such as restaurants, cafes, bars and shopping malls.

Apartments also cater to a wide range of end users, from young professionals to investors and university students to downsizers. They can be used as Airbnbs, as secondary residences – the list goes on!

Apartment complexes can house amenities such as pools, gyms, co-working spaces, rooftop spaces and outdoor spaces. In addition, the ground floor can accommodate shops that not only service passing foot traffic but also the residents above; we touch on this later when we discuss commercial and retail property.

Holding

As with townhouses, apartment complexes attract body corporate or strata fees. These are paid by the owner of each respective unit. The scale of these types of developments can be large, so holding costs can be significant. These types of developments where residual stock are held are more common with well-known companies such as Meriton and Mirvac.

Selling

Again, selling apartments is about understanding the demand for each product you're developing. Holding onto the premium stock with better views or more bedrooms and living spaces will help you to yield the highest margin possible and prevent you having to reduce prices significantly on lower-quality stock in the apartment building. Unlike townhouse projects, you can't stagger the release of an apartment building (which is when you sell a portion and potentially hold off from developing the rest to sell later); it's effectively one building, so you'll need to complete it to sell it!

Steve and Liam's tips

There are two uses for the word 'staging' in development-speak. In this chapter we refer to staging, meaning selling apartments at different stages of the development. The other use of the word staging refers to when you set a property up for sale. See chapter 13 for more on staging your property to maximise your sale price.

CHAPTER TWO
COMMERCIAL

Commercial properties typically generate two to three times the cash flow of their residential counterparts. To learn the ins and outs of commercial property, please see Steve's first book *Commercial Property Investing Explained Simply*.

Property types

Let's look at the different types of commercial property, and then we'll move on to the considerations for holding or selling commercial property.

Industrial

There is a wide range of uses for industrial property, including warehousing and distribution, workshops, cold storage, corporate storage, man caves – the list goes on. The scale of industrial properties can differ too, from small strata complexes with owners or tenants that are small and medium-sized enterprises (SMEs) to large multinational distributors. The construction of these types of buildings can vary from the typical concrete tilt panel warehouses, to metal-clad sheds, to large laydown areas with either gravel or concrete hardstand.

The ecommerce boom has increased the popularity of, and therefore demand for, these types of assets. The future outlook for this sector is very promising. Industrial land is at a premium now, so understanding where local councils plan to potentially rezone rural land to industrial land can be extremely lucrative.

Retail

As with industrial property, retail property has a wide range of asset and build types, ranging from suburban strip shops to large shopping centres. They can even be a combination of residential and commercial (commercial on the ground floor, residential on top; Steve coined the term 'resimercial', which is now common terminology in the market). The location of these developments is extremely important, as owner-occupiers and tenants rely on foot traffic and exposure for their businesses to be successful. Also, amenities such as car parking are critical for both staff and customers.

Understanding your target market is arguably more critical for retail property than industrial property. The best-case scenario is to have a precommitment from a business to lease or purchase; this then allows the project to be designed specifically to meet their needs. The risk of prolonged vacancy is higher in retail property than industrial property at the time of writing, so mitigating this risk is extremely important in the early phases of the development.

Offices

Offices involve a similar construction process to apartments. They're typically located close to CBDs or infrastructure such as train stations or car parks. Offices can be low-rise in outer suburbs or regional locations, or multi-storey, mixed-use developments that house national and international businesses such as major banks, insurance companies, IT companies and government departments.

Office projects often take years to be approved and even longer to construct, especially those typically in CBDs that are 50-plus storeys high. The funding for these projects can come from sources other than traditional bank lending, such as private investors or mezzanine finance (see chapter 10 for more on this). As with retail developments, having precommitted tenants or owners for these buildings is a huge risk mitigator for these types of projects.

Since COVID-19, office-space vacancy rates in Australia have shot up to around 15 per cent; there is the least amount of demand for this asset class at the time of writing due to oversupply. However, there are always opportunities in the market, as you may be able to pick up a site at a bargain price.

Hold or sell?

The considerations for holding or selling commercial property are largely the same across the different types, although there are some considerations that are specific to certain types of commercial property.

Holding

Holding commercial property is like having your cake and eating it too! The net returns are much higher than for residential property. The tenants in these properties will generally pay all the outgoings, so all that's left for you to do is collect the rent. The rent will typically cover your expenses, such as interest and insurances, and build a significant passive income if that is your strategy long term.

Generally, the purpose of holding commercial stock is either to build this passive income for your retirement or to create another income stream to assist with financing future projects. Capital growth can come, but the priority should be the cash flow generated. Income from developments is lumpy – you get paid large chunks of money upon completion – so having a more consistent income stream is beneficial from a lending perspective.

How much stock you can hold will depend on your financing. If you use debt to develop the project, this will need to be paid out first through a portion of the sales, and the residual stock can then be held or sold off as profit. It's also very important from an accounting perspective that you're clear about your intention with the overall project. Once you know that you plan to hold all or part of the site, you can advise your accountant so they can provide the correct tax structuring.

In commercial, the main risk is vacancy and finding tenants to lease the property. Holding onto vacant property is cash intensive due to holding costs such as interest, insurances, strata fees, utilities and council rates. This makes it very important to have a good understanding of potential owner-occupiers' or tenants' fit-out requirements. It can be market-dependent as to who is responsible for this fit-out. In a hot market, the tenant will be happy to secure a blank space and complete the fit-out themselves so they can commence the operation of their business quickly. Alternatively, you may need to offer incentives or fit-out contributions to incoming tenants or even owner-occupiers. For example, a tenant may require three months to complete their fit-out before they can commence operating their business and will therefore want three months rent-free as an incentive to sign a new lease; or, you could offer to pay for the fit-out in exchange for the tenant paying rent from day one.

Different commercial property types have different risk profiles for vacancy. At the time of writing, industrial properties have their lowest vacancy rates in history, with most capital cities being under 2 per cent. On the other hand, the risk and length of vacancy is much higher for office space off the back of COVID-19; the hybrid work-from-home movement appears to be here to stay, and we're seeing the space required for office users reduce as a result.

However, in today's market offices fetch the highest yield of any commercial property type. Yield will be dictated by the terms of the lease you secure on the property: the length of the lease, rental increases, options for the tenant to extend the lease beyond the current term, and the security on the lease.

Selling

There are two main markets to sell to in commercial property: owner-occupiers and investors.

When selling to investors, you'll likely need to secure a lease first to then market the property as a 'leased investment'. Some investors are happy to purchase vacant, but the vast majority will require a lease in place for finance purposes. Also, the buyer will typically be required to pay GST on the purchase price if the property is vacant, so they'll need to come up with this extra 10 per cent in addition to their deposit (although they will get this back on their first business activity statement, or BAS).

The terms of the lease are very important, as stronger terms mean a higher sale price. For example, a national tenant on a ten-year lease with options is much more valuable than a small business with a three-year lease. In addition, the quality of the tenant is important – for example, medical consulting rooms with a large, expensive fit-out will fetch a higher price than a hair salon.

Your other option is to offer a 'rental guarantee' or 'leaseback'. This is where you pay the rent on a unit or building for a pre-determined period, such as 12 months, which can assist in selling to investors. This can be particularly advantageous when owner-occupier demand has dried up and you have leftover stock that you can sell quickly to investors, instead of waiting around to find a tenant and then selling once a lease is signed. Once the buyer obtains a tenant, the 'leaseback' will typically be removed. See *Commercial Property Investing Explained Simply* for a full understanding of how leases work.

Understanding the level of demand from owner-occupiers and investors and having a clear idea from the outset of which type of buyer you are targeting is key to quickly selling stock for the target price or above. Some regions have a much higher demand for owner-occupiers and others are investor playgrounds.

The size of the property can also be a factor. Typically, small businesses want to own their (smaller) property because of the tax advantages. The larger the space is, the less likely the tenant will want to own it, as larger companies are not typically in the property game and are instead focused on their profits and growth.

Consulting with local property managers, selling agents or even buyer's agents about the best target market can help you de-risk this critical part of the process. This should be done at the initial stage of the development and prior to signing contracts, as the decision to either hold or sell will dictate what structuring you put in place. You can also de-risk by having a precommitment with a buyer before construction, as you'll be working with them directly on the fit-out until completion and the eventual sale.

CHAPTER THREE
SPECIALTY

While the development types covered in chapters 1 and 2 are the most common, there are several other specialty types of development.

Boarding houses

Boarding or rooming houses are a single dwelling with multiple occupants who each occupy a room and share communal facilities such as kitchen, bathroom and living spaces. It's important to note that if there are more than 20 residents, an on-site manager is required.

There is different legislation that applies to boarding houses in each state. For example, in New South Wales, you must comply with the *Boarding Houses Act 2012* and *Boarding Houses Regulation 2013*. The key reasons this legislation is in place are to establish a public register of boarding houses in NSW, to allow local councils to inspect these properties for compliance, to introduce occupancy rights for people living in boarding houses and to be more accommodating for people with additional needs.

In NSW, general boarding houses accommodate five or more paying residents (not including the proprietor, the manager and members of their families). Assisted boarding houses accommodate two or more persons with additional needs. These assisted boarding houses are licensed by the NSW Department of Communities and Justice, and the occupants have additional support or supervision with daily tasks such as personal care, preparing meals and managing medication.

Boarding or rooming houses are generally most successful near universities or even in mining towns. Residents can be quite transient, and these types of properties cater well to this market. Developers can potentially increase their success by adding more specific requirements to the property, such as ensuite bathrooms for each bedroom, which can increase the returns.

Holding

These types of assets are great for cash flow and provide diverse income streams. The key factor is maintaining compliance with the legislation. To be placed on the Boarding House Register, details such as the property address, the boarding house proprietor, the definition of the boarding house and the local council area all need to be confirmed.

Management of these types of properties is also critical. The general maintenance costs can be much higher, as can the turnover of tenants, which means lots of advertising for new residents. If this isn't managed well, the returns can be reduced significantly.

Selling

The market for properties of this type will most likely be investors: either those who manage and live in the property themselves or who will employ someone to manage the property on their behalf.

How does GST work?

As with all property developments, there are GST implications to consider. Boarding houses are classed as commercial residential premises and are therefore not input-taxed. The sale will be a taxable supply unless it's classed as a 'going concern'. Your accountant will be able to confirm these details when it comes time to sell. See chapter 10 for more information on GST.

Special needs housing

Special needs housing comprises specific properties that cater for people with extreme functional impairment or very high needs. There are four types of specialist disability accommodation (SDA): Improved Liveability, Fully Accessible, High Physical Support and Robust. Here are some features to consider when designing these types of projects:

- Enhanced provisions for people with sensory, intellectual or cognitive impairment
- Power supply for doors and windows, and automation for sinks, benches and appliances
- Resilient materials that can reduce the risk of injury and cope with heavy use
- Structural provisions for ceiling hoists
- 950mm wide openings for doors to all habitable rooms
- Communications technology
- Emergency power solutions to cater for a minimum two-hour power outage if the welfare of the resident/s is at risk.

The designs of these properties are very specific to suit a particular resident or disability. This is critical, and therefore the demand for the property must be researched well and confirmed. If designed well, the resident can be there long term, which is an extremely rewarding outcome for all parties.

Holding

Securing a long-term tenant for a property of this type can make it an extremely high-yielding investment. The cash flow will rival some of the best commercial investments. The main risk with holding is that if the tenant were to leave, you would effectively be holding a very expensive house. If a tenant can't be secured under the NDIS and the property is leased to the general market, the returns will be significantly lower and the value of the property will reduce.

Selling

Special needs housing can be sold directly to the future occupant. This can be extremely rewarding for both parties as you have developed a property that will significantly improve their life. There is also the potential for this 'sale' to occur early on when the future occupant can have input into the development to suit their exact needs. This is like an off-the-plan contract.

The alternative is to sell the property to an investor looking for a high-cash-flow investment. The length of the tenure will determine the potential value of the property, much like with commercial property.

Specialised commercial property

Purpose-built, specialised commercial property includes hotels, car wash stations, petrol stations, cinemas, funeral homes and community halls. One of the benefits of specialised commercial is that properties typically come with very long leases. As the tenants have fewer options to change their location easily due to very minimal stock, they desire the security of a long lease and lots of options on that lease. Finance is typically harder for these properties, and you need to understand the specialised asset you choose very carefully.

One of the most common and attractive specialised assets for developers is child care centres.

Child care centres

Child care is now an established and essential part of Australia's education system. Demand and expectations of care are increasing year on year, so it's critical that child care centres continue to develop, evolve curriculums and provide high-quality, safe spaces for occupants. The design needs to be considered carefully so that it meets planning and licensing regulations. Site suitability analysis is extremely important, and developers can access companies that specialise in modelling, designing and completing feasibilities for potential child care sites.

In addition, child care centres are highly sought-after assets for investors as they are underpinned by significant government support. The value of these assets comes down to a combination of factors, such as the age of property, the length of the lease, the provider, the number of children it can accommodate, the location and the style of property (such as whether it is a freestanding building or part of an office building). The simplest way to calculate the potential value of a site is using the capitalisation (cap) rate method, similar to commercial property: divide the projected net income by the projected cap rate. For example, a site that can cater for 100 children (at $4500 per child) in a location that attracts a 5 per cent cap rate would be worth $9 million.

Developers can either convert an existing site to child care or, if the zoning allows, construct a new property to facilitate future use as a child care centre. It's important to note that when converting an older property, there are a number of requirements that need to be catered for, such as parking, access, internal amenities, and privacy and security measures.

As with most specialised assets, child care commands long leases. Unlike industrial, their success is completely tied to the location of the property, so they will want the security of long leases and lots of options.

You can typically work with future tenants to assist with the fit-out costs, and in return receive a higher yield, or some form of longer lease or payback method.

Holding

Just like commercial property, developing child care centres can be extremely lucrative. As you're developing these properties at raw cost and then holding the income, the returns are much greater than purchasing a completed site. The security of a long lease is also very attractive and can result in a high-yielding and secure asset.

The capacity to hold the property will be your biggest challenge, as these types of projects are capital-intensive. Long term, you'll also need to consider the longevity of the site and its provider. If you lost the tenant in the future, the value of the property would drop significantly.

Selling

The best time to sell a child care centre may not necessarily be when it's first completed and a tenant commences their long-term lease. Most often you'll need to offer an incentive for at least the first year until the tenant/operator is up and running at capacity, which will reduce your income for that year. Investors will see this as a negative and likely request the price be reduced or the rent shortfall be paid out.

You'll need to calculate year on year as you receive income (and factor in rental increases) if you're better off holding the property, receiving income and then selling at a later stage. This is a function of your total cash inflows upon completion (borrowings, cash and rental income) versus your total cash outflows (interest, land tax, insurances and selling costs). It may be better to hold the property until the fifth year, receiving income up until that point, and then sell, as the income over that timeframe plus the increased sale price will be higher than just the sale price in the first year.

CHAPTER FOUR
TITLES

Just as there are several types of property you can develop, there are several types of titles, depending on the property. In Australia, the most common type of property title is Torrens title or 'freehold'. This means you're buying the land and the property (or just the land alone) and that the property belongs to the title owner – you. A Torrens title is legally binding and enforceable by law. This type of title was first developed and named by Sir Robert Torrens in 1863 after more than 40,000 land grants vanished in the 1800s.

This chapter explains other types of titles.

Strata

Strata title is usually a title for one of several units within the same construction. You might see a property referred to as 'strata-titled' or just 'strata'. It means that you own one apartment and everything within it, but everything outside your dwelling – such as communal grounds, gardens and facilities – is usually owned and maintained by the managing authority (the body corporate or owners' corporation) and paid for through a maintenance fee.

Community

Community title is a little less well known. A good way to conceptualise it is as the halfway point between a Torrens title and a strata title: you own your parcel of the land, but you also own a section of what is deemed 'community' or 'common' property. This could be something as small as a garden bed or as large as a driveway or swimming pool.

Company

Company title simply signifies that a company owns the title to the land. Buying a certain number of shares in the corporation means that the shareholder is entitled to the exclusive use and occupation of a unit and shared use of any common property.

Less common titles

Less common titles include Limited Torrens (where there aren't clear boundaries to the property), leasehold (which applies to government-owned land leased for 99 years rather than being sold) and old system (for properties existing before Torrens title, although these are hard to find).

Finding out about property titles

How do you find out about a property's title? It depends which state or territory the property is in. Your conveyancer or solicitor can assist you. This table provides a general guide.

Finding out about property titles by state/territory

State/Territory	Platform
ACT	You can access property information at the Access Canberra website (accesscanberra.act.gov.au). However, to do searches and access titles, you'll need to visit a local Office of Regulatory Services or the Environment, Planning and Sustainable Development Directorate in Dickson. There's also an online subscription service option for a fee.
NSW	Various platforms exist, including Morris Hayes & Edgar (MHE), Direct Info, Hazlett Information Services, LegalStream, GlobalX and Intertek Inform (previously SAI Global).
NT	No free online title searches are available at this point, so head to a Land Titles Office or request a phone search: call 08 8999 6520. There is an online portal for professionals with a monthly subscription fee.
Qld	You can look up titles at qld.gov.au/environment/land/title for a small fee.
SA	Head to sailis.lssa.com.au, which allows you to search as a guest without having an account. A small fee is payable for a property search.
Tas.	Head to thelist.tas.gov.au and pay a small fee, and you'll be able to do a straightforward search.
Vic.	Head to www.landata.online and pay a small fee to access easy-to-find information.
WA	Head to landgate.wa.gov.au and pay a small fee to do a property search.

PART III
BEGINNING A PROPERTY DEVELOPMENT

A rmed with your understanding of the types of properties that comprise the large umbrella of the development industry, you may be wondering how all the pieces of the puzzle fit together.

Unlike buying and selling property to invest, property development is complex. The process of creating a property from scratch involves many steps and moving parts, and these are all impacted by different elements depending on the unique aspects of each development. For example, a flood overlay will require more engineering consultancy work (and potentially a lower selling price if in a flood zone), or objections to your building application can result in more solicitors and design fees as the project is reiterated.

In other words, no development is the same and no timeline is standard. This means that following a paint-by-numbers approach can be tricky – more steps means more opportunities for things to pop up and change your plans.

However, regardless of the type of property, there IS a general process you can follow. By understanding the bigger picture and how all the moving parts are connected, you'll be able to see what comes next generally and how a development is achievable from start to finish. Embarking on a property development is more complicated than buying and selling, but while each variable can and often does change due to the unpredictable nature of developments, developers every day around the world are completing projects. You can too!

Our general seven-step process, and some rough estimates of the timeline for each step, is as follows:

1. **Find the site (2 to 4 months).** This starts with area research and becoming the local expert in understanding what product is in demand, the future supply of this product, what it costs to

build and what it will sell for. It then involves searching for the best site with the highest use. People always look for a unicorn and can search for years (and never find it). Be realistic with your returns so you can get stuck into a deal! Keep in mind that markets are subject to change, so you need to understand where future supply and demand will be.

2. **Complete initial feasibility (3 to 4 hours).** This back-of-the-envelope study should only require a few hours of your time, but skipping this step can be the difference between failure and success.

3. **Complete detailed feasibility (1 to 2 weeks).** This is when you start to have advanced discussions with town planners, architects, builders, engineers, surveyors, sales agents and financiers or brokers. They will give you a more detailed breakdown of the costs involved, along with any potential issues with the site that you'll need to overcome. (Note, it's not uncommon for detailed feasibility to render a site no longer viable if one of your consultants picks up something that restricts the site or reduces profit. Even if you have to pay a small fee to some of these consultants at this stage, it's well and truly worth it to avoid pursuing a dud site!)

4. **Organise conveyancing, finance and buying structures (2 to 4 weeks).** If your detailed feasibility looks good, you can sort out all the conveyancing, finance and buying structures involved with the property development. Conveyancing will come back into play at the end of the project, and finance can continue through the entire project, but it typically takes two to four weeks to get the ball rolling. It usually takes one or two days for the conveyancer to review the contract, noting it can be subject to due diligence or finance, and option agreements may take longer to be generated and reviewed. As for finance, this is when your broker will take your feasibility and shop

it around to potential lenders to confirm they'll lend to the project. Also, depending on the state or territory you're purchasing in, you'll likely need to confirm your buying structure before you sign the contract.

5. **Buy the site (1 to 4 weeks; BIGFIG 1: What are you buying the site for?).** Now it's time to test your negotiation skills. This is all about understanding how to structure your best offer with regard to price and terms. The negotiation can be quite quick (less than one week), especially if you're in the position to put an offer forward unconditionally. If you're looking to secure the site under an option agreement, expect the legal paperwork to take one or two weeks to be drawn up. Add another one or two weeks for the vendor to review with their legal team and come back to you with any potential changes.

6. **Build your development (18 months to 3 years; BIGFIG 2: What will it cost to build the development?).** This is the longest part of the process and can take up to three years. There are varying stages within this process depending on the size of the project. First, the development approval process can vary in length dramatically depending on the local council, anywhere from three to nine months. The next step is to obtain your building permit or construction certificate, which could take another three to six months depending on how complex the project is and the level of engineering input required. Only once you have these can you finally commence construction. Again, depending on the size of the project, this can vary from 9 to 18 months (or longer for high-rise apartments, for example).

7. **Make your money (2 to 4 months; BIGFIG 3: What will you sell it for?).** Once your development is finished and you're preparing for the next step, you'll need to organise the titles, which can take up to two months. At the same time, you'll be

preparing to settle off-the-plan sales or continue marketing and selling your completed product. Allowing for standard settlement timeframes, this could take another one to two months once titles have been issued.

You'll see we have introduced three Big Figures, or BIGFIGs, as we like to call them. As you read on, you'll see that these are the most crucial pieces of the puzzle for any developer. They're the questions any good developer starts with when contemplating a project, and while they do fit within other steps – and you'll see them pop up throughout the book – they stand alone too. The BIGFIGs are also the basis for initial feasibility, which you'll read about in chapter 5.

Part III takes you through the initial steps and your first crucial big-picture considerations before going any further. We also share with you the people you need in your corner – your foundation team. Building the right team is crucial to your success; these will be the people you're trusting with your money, so it's vital they have the right experience and expertise to make your project a success. Keep in mind that these processes, timelines and team are all general and are easily subject to change, depending on your needs at the time.

We hope to inspire you to believe in your ability to take on a project with confidence. The only way is up!

CHAPTER FIVE
FINDING THE SITE AND INITIAL FEASIBILITY

When it comes to finding a site, you may have heard the term 'highest and best use'. We introduced you to this phrase earlier, and it's possibly the most important set of words about finding success in property development – other than 'profit', of course! It means working out the best use of the land and what will yield the most profit.

Think about it: why would a developer build a house on a beachfront block that's better suited to luxury apartments? That's not utilising the land's highest and best use; building the house means leaving hundreds of thousands of dollars on the table. Likewise, why build a set of seven townhouses when you could easily build eight? Again, this could make the deal unprofitable and not worth doing. Why would you not maximise the best use of the land with all development sites? (This doesn't mean that you should be cramming as many townhouses into a block as possible; what if three high-end houses are more profitable than six townhouses?)

To determine the best-use cases and best profitability for a site, you need to do your due diligence. As with our first two books, due diligence is the most important part of property development. But unlike commercial and residential property, where you simply buy or sell land or a property, development requires a whole other suite of competencies (of which buying and selling also play a part, depending on your strategy).

Due diligence is highly comprehensive because it includes detailed feasibility, outlining the specifics of what needs to take place throughout the development, when, who's involved and how to move onto the next stage. It's essential to do this work because it will determine whether what you want to develop will achieve its highest and best use, and help you achieve your goals. The purpose of due diligence is to discover current or potential problems across the broad spectrum of a development's timeline, understand its upside and verify the information obtained. This will help you see the big picture as to the project's viability – in vivid detail.

A free checklist to help you conduct due diligence is available for download at paliseproperty.com.

Once you know what you want to achieve, and you understand what potential buyers are looking for in completed developments and how much demand there is, you're ready to start site-hunting. As we've discussed, choosing the right site means making sure it aligns with your goals, which you should have already worked through in Part I.

Start reaching out to selling agents and let them know what you're looking for. Other ways to get sites include letterbox-dropping and doorknocking. Buyer's agents can also be a great source for finding sites. Note that not all suburbs and areas will provide profitable feasibilities; if the numbers don't work in a given location for a certain project, move on to the next one.

Initial feasibility

Once you're interested in a piece of land and think you might like to develop it, it's time to put down some numbers. This is sometimes known as an 'initial feasibility' or 'back-of-an-envelope' study. It's a high-level way to quickly check out all aspects of a site to ensure it will be viable for the project, and it's a way to get you **thinking** like a professional developer. All developers will do one of these as a quick assessment of whether a project's worth pursuing. The key is that it starts to formalise your intentions and provide a sense of whether what you're proposing will stack up.

This is the first step towards bringing your development to life. You'll need to sit down and allow a few hours for this. It involves adding up hypothetical numbers (costs) and understanding what price range you can sell for once the development is completed. This is also usually the first thing you'll do before you can negotiate with the selling agent. It's always good to get a rough idea of the site purchase price from the agent first if you can.

To run your initial feasibility, start with the three BIGFIGs we mentioned in the introduction to this part:

1. What are you buying the site for?
2. What will it cost to build the development?
3. What will you sell it for?

This will give you three numbers: land price, build cost and sale price. If you understand these figures, you can save lots of time and make quick decisions to secure a potential site that stacks up. If you always start by asking these three critical questions, you'll start thinking like a developer. In Part II, we covered the various property development types and whether to hold or sell them, and the pros and cons of each; now, as a developer, your next step is to consider a piece of land and work out what you're going to do with it.

It's important to remember that if you get these three BIGFIGs wrong, it doesn't matter how accurate the other smaller numbers are – you'll be in trouble. We can't tell you how often people have come to us for our take on ads they've seen online for a development, and 90 per cent of them don't stack up. That's why they're being advertised! Had the back of the envelope study been done, the development wouldn't have needed to be online for sale.

These initial calculations will give you a solid foundation from which to grow. It doesn't mean that the development will be a success, but at least you'll know whether to stop or go before getting in too deep.

Let's look at each of these questions in a little more detail.

BIGFIG 1: What are you buying the site for?

Understand the local council regulations and find out what types of developments are allowed by the property's zoning and site coverage. Get a town planner to help you understand what can occupy the block while abiding by council regulations, market needs and the costs to complete the project. Essentially, you want to determine the highest selling price minus costs for any given piece of land. Don't make the mistake of not assessing the land's full potential.

BIGFIG 2: What will it cost to build the development?

Consider the condition of the site and the work that will be required to build the development. Is there anything that needs to be cleared, such as trees or existing structures? Are there any access issues, such as a bus shelter or power pole in front of the site? Are there existing utilities and services connected to the site, and can you access them? Are there any overlays? Is the block sloping, and will this result in more earthworks, retaining walls or foundation work?

What finishes are you looking to complete? Will the development be high-end and targeting owner-occupiers, or low- to mid-spec and targeting investors or first-home buyers?

Determine the demographics of the area, who aspires to live there and what types of services or amenities attract buyers to the location. For example, if you're building a townhouse complex aimed at families, it might be a good plan to include a pool, but if you're building a 50s-and-over retirement complex, a pool might be less attractive. Another example is that if you're building in an expensive, blue-chip area, the demographic there may prefer high-end finishes and be prepared to pay for them; this might not work in an affordable suburb, where you won't get a return on the extra cost to add those fittings and fixtures. Aim to design a project that fits with the region and is targeted at the market you have identified for the area.

Fitting out bathrooms and kitchens can be a minefield for the uninitiated. When it comes to sinks, undermount benches are more expensive. Splashbacks and tiling add to expenses too, while lighting also presents challenges.

Here are some questions you could ask agents:

- Do buyers want tiled floors throughout, or wooden flooring?
- Do they want 20 mm or 40 mm benchtops?
- Do they want waterfall edges?
- Do they want drop-down pendants over island benches, or downlights in all living areas?
- What size tiles do they prefer in wet areas?
- Are lifts essential, or can you just put provisions for a lift to be installed in the future?
- Are walk-in pantries (WIPs) a must-have or a nice-to-have?

If you don't know what any of these mean, get out there and get educated!

Fundamental build costs across an area will generally stay the same whether you build in a lower-socioeconomic area or an affluent area. It's key to understand what the end value will be as this is what can make or break a profitable project.

BIGFIG 3: What will you sell it for?

Determine comparable sales by researching on-market properties (using real estate websites like REA, Domain or paid websites such as CoreLogic) or off-market properties (by speaking to local selling agents who sell the type of property you're hoping to develop). Compare similar properties to your proposed development located as close as possible to the site (or at least within the same suburb). Ensure they're truly comparable in terms of the size of the property, its age, its fixtures and so on. The value can drop significantly if you're one block from the beach versus three blocks back, for example.

Proximity to amenities, parks, schools and public transport will have an impact on the selling price, as will whether your site is in the 'good' or 'bad' part of town. This might not be visible on a map, so ask around. Don't expect the best price for properties in a 'bad' location, such as if they back onto a train line or are next to a housing commission development. In general, it's better to focus on the good parts of town, as they will attract buyers who are emotionally attached and want to pay more. Similarly, they will grow more in value, attract a higher rent and be easier to find tenants for if you choose to hold the property. However, it's always case by case; sometimes the 'bad' areas of town have shorter days on market and are in more demand, so if the development is profitable and it's easier to sell, you can still be onto a winner.

In our experience, it's best to know what the market wants and then give it to them. Know your area and become the local expert. Know exactly what raw sites sell for, as well as two-bedroom and three-bedroom townhouses, and even high-end duplexes. Go to inspections, speak with agents, get to grips with what people are talking about – what buyers like and what standard finishes and inclusions they're willing to pay more for.

***

We've broken down these considerations into a handy checklist. You can also find a free download of this checklist at paliseproperty.com.

BIGFIG 1: What are you buying the site for?	
Size	
What is the land area of the site?	
What is the minimum lot size required?	
Frontage	
What is the frontage of the site?	
Zoning	
Is the site suitably zoned?	
What product will the zoning allow?	
Apartments	
Townhouses	
Dual occupancy	
Subdivision	
Industrial units	
Mixed-use	
Yield	
What is the expected yield for apartments?	
What is the expected yield for townhouses?	
What is the expected yield for dual occupancy?	
What is the expected yield for subdivision?	

What is the expected yield for industrial units?	
What is the expected yield for mixed-use?	
Height	
What height will the zoning allow?	
BIGFIG 2: What will it cost to build the development?	
Site features	
Does the site require civil works, such as earthworks and retaining walls?	
Does the site neighbour any properties that can inhibit development, such as service stations, high-rise apartments or heritage-listed properties?	
Does the site require clearing? If so, do you require an arborist report?	
Does the site have acid sulphate soils or deep soil zones? If so, is there additional ground treatment required?	
Are there neighbouring trees where the root zone impacts the site?	
Is there any demolition of existing dwellings or structures required? If so, is there asbestos present?	
Does the site require external works to facilitate the development, such as widening of roads, or additional kerb, gutter or footpaths?	
Utilities/services	
Is there an existing telecommunications connection to the site?	
Is there an existing sewer connection to the site? If yes, is it downstream of the new dwellings? If not, do you require a sewer pump, and does the council allow for sewer pumps to be used?	

Is there an existing water connection to the site?	
Is there an existing electricity connection to the site?	
Is there an existing gas connection to the site?	
Is there an existing NBN connection to the site?	
Is there an existing stormwater connection to the site?	
If there is an existing stormwater connection, is it downstream of the new dwellings? (Stormwater can't be pumped like sewer water.)	
If there is not an existing stormwater connection, can you discharge stormwater through an adjacent property or land? If so, is this a registered easement that an entitlement could be gained for?	
Overlays	
Does the site have a flood overlay? If so, to what extent (low, medium, high risk)? Is there a reduced level (RL) for floor level that provides flood immunity?	
Does the site have overland flow overlay (i.e. new buildings can't impede flow)?	
Does the site have any heritage overlays?	
Does the site have any bushfire overlays?	
Does the site have any environmental overlays?	
Does the site have any demolition control overlays?	
Other	
Are there any power poles and/or low overhanging cables that impede current or future access?	
Are there any physical bus shelters or structures that impede current or future access?	
Are there any communication pits in the verge? If so, how shallow are the cables, and will they require lowering?	

BIGFIG 3: What will you sell it for?	
Land size	
What do properties with a similar lot size sell for?	
What is the proportion of backyard to building area?	
Build size	
What do properties with a similar internal build area sell for?	
Are there additional areas, such as balconies, voids or double garages?	
Specifications	
Low-, medium- or high-spec finishes?	
Number of bathrooms	
Checking the number of bedrooms of similar properties, is there a big jump in price from three-bedroom to four-bedroom, or four-bedroom with a study versus five bedrooms?	
Flooring quality: tiled, timber or carpet?	
Location	
Proximity to schools	
Proximity to public transport	
Proximity to services such as shops, cafes and restaurants	
Proximity to amenities such as beaches, parks or other open space	
Aspect	
What direction does it face? (In Australia, north-facing is always preferred.)	
What views do other comparable sales have?	

You'll note, if you jump ahead to the next chapter, that this initial feasibility forms the basis for the larger puzzle of detailed feasibility. This is intentional to keep the steps as simple as possible, and for you to only consider what you need to at this early stage. If you consider detailed feasibility the fleshed-out version of initial feasibility, it might help you to see the whole picture holistically in your head.

CHAPTER SIX
DETAILED FEASIBILITY

Detailed feasibility is a detailed analysis of whether the project is 'feasible' and worth doing, considering the risks and opportunity cost. As an extension of initial feasibility, this requires you to talk to your team and get quotes, so allow a few weeks and be prepared to pay money (including for a few coffees!) for this part.

Whereas initial feasibility involves running hypothetical costs, detailed feasibility uses exact costs (or as close as possible). You get these exact costs by talking to the respective team member who will have a detailed look at the site and give you their quote. In the Palise Property office, we fill out a spreadsheet for the detailed feasibility of every single property development we assess.

Why is detailed feasibility important?

Detailed feasibility is a core part of the property development process. It's your responsibility, as part of the due diligence process, to bring together all the costs, people, paperwork and outcomes, enabling you to account for each contingency and prepare for the next.

It includes the acquisition and development costs (including financing), but also development approvals. This means knowing what you can build on the site and what zoning and planning approvals will be greenlit by that specific local council. It's also important to factor in any council contributions to be paid as part of the project, along with any other government-related fees.

What's involved

We've covered initial feasibility and the typical timeline for a development from start to finish. These are small cogs of a much bigger wheel, which we flesh out in more detail here. Think of this as your blueprint for property development. Note that the list below is not meant to be exhaustive as there may be other consultants required, but this offers a general guide of what to expect and some of the more common requirements.

These are the eight typical detailed feasibility stages, or key costs:

1. Acquiring your site (BIGFIG 1).
2. Securing your permits and/or construction certificates.
3. Organising your finance.
4. Building your development (BIGFIG 2).
5. Holding costs or income.
6. Registering your titles.
7. Marketing and selling your development.
8. Making your money (BIGFIG 3).

By the end, you should have your projected costs, profit margin and margin of safety.

Once you understand the dependencies, you can start building the pieces of the puzzle by managing your cash flow and your timeline. Developments can take anywhere from one to three years to complete from start to finish, and you'll need to map out each dependency to keep track of what you need to do next. Remember to lean on your team to secure accurate quotes for each of the eight steps.

Acquiring your site

This is the first of the three BIGFIGs! We covered how to find a site in the previous chapter, but when it comes to feasibility, this is when you need to put the numbers down and reiterate what you are willing to purchase the site for. It can be the hardest and most time-consuming part of all developments. The timing can vary and will depend on how well you can negotiate. A longer settlement with conditions will allow you time to complete (and hopefully de-risk) some of the following development and building permit items, which can save a lot of interest costs:

- **Legal structure.** We cover this in more detail in chapter 11, but in short, the legal structure you choose will be dependent on what you plan to do with the site once you've bought and developed it: hold or sell. Defining your goals, as we discussed earlier in the book, will help you to work this out. The legal structure for a trust or company, for example, will cost between $2000 and $5000 to set up.

- **Conveyancing.** Conveyancing fees can also vary and will depend on the complexity of the contract. Fees can vary from a few thousand dollars to upwards of $10,000. Your conveyancer will become involved as you're about to secure contracts on a site, just as in a residential or commercial transaction.

- **Stamp duty.** Stamp duty is a tax charged on the transfer of land. Each state and territory has their own fee structure. You can estimate the stamp duty on each state or territory's government website using their online calculator. You can also access a free copy of the Palise Property stamp duty calculator on our website. This will be a large chunk of money, so take the time to calculate it correctly. Your conveyancer will also be able to assist you in confirming this figure closer to settlement. Stamp duty will be payable at settlement.

Securing your permits and/or construction certificate

Once you have secured your site, the next step is to organise your permits, which will allow you to legally carry out construction on your site. You'll need a minimum of two permits: one for development and another for building or construction. This step can be time-consuming, because there are many moving parts involved and you're at the mercy of the local council. That's not including if there are objections to your permit, which is a whole other ball game.

Securing your permits means securing reports from a long list of consultants too, depending on how relevant they are for your development.

Land surveyor

The land surveyor will measure and chart the boundaries of your land. They will help identify property boundaries, capture elevation and terrain data, and map existing utilities to support site planning with precise measurements.

The survey will be one of their first tasks, as the architect will require this information to commence their concept. It will include all of the surroundings, such as the slope and contours of the site, all dimensions of the existing house, trees, and any infrastructure or existing services and easements. They also need to locate anything outside of the site, such as manholes, stormwater pits, other utilities and overhead services. Neighbouring properties are also important, including setbacks and window locations.

Town planner

The earlier you can engage a town planner, the better, as their role is one of the most important. Even if it costs you a small fee (up to $500), it's worth it to get them to provide high-level guidance on what is likely to get approved. It can also result in you not wasting time on a site that is unlikely to stack up. Time wasted on a deal that won't progress is time you could have spent looking for another deal, so value your time well!

Essentially, town planners understand local regulations and requirements and can guide you on the highest and best use for the development. They provide guidance on planning schemes and will have intimate knowledge of what will be permitted on a site given the zoning. Similar to an architect, they will know what projects are getting approved and what is working well from a development perspective.

Beyond that, they will then help to negotiate with local planning authorities to obtain permission for your development. Similar to agents, town planners charge a fee based on the complexity of the project and the time required for the planning approval.

Architect / building designer

The architect or building designer designs the building and comes up with floor plans. They're involved early on, potentially even prior to securing a site. Good architects will have inside information as to what projects are working in a certain location. Other consultants will be relying on the architect's information, so it's critical that they start early and you can keep them to an agreed timeline. Some architects can complete town planning too.

The difference between a good architect and a great architect is their commercial understanding. A great architect will help you achieve the largest possible premium by designing a dwelling that not only looks good but is also desired by the target demographic.

They can also come up with 'massing plans', which will determine what is possible for a potential site (for example, how many units you can build on the land). A good architect will have a solid understanding of the council guidelines to comply with the planning scheme. The plans and design will include dimensions and cross-sections, which engineers will need to review to provide their assessments.

Once your development is built, they will also certify completion of the building work.

Their fees will be determined by the size of the project, and they're often paid a fee based on the percentage of the total building contract sum. In addition, their fees will be spread across this stage of the development and the subsequent building permit stage.

Engineers

Your engineer will work with the architect and the quantity surveyor to advise on the design elements of your development. You'll need reports for your development from a number of different types of engineers, depending on what's critical to your site:

- **Acoustic engineers** specialise in how sound travels – and, more specifically for property development, how to prevent it from travelling. Acoustic reports may be required if the development is near a flight path, busy roads or trains. Fees will be highly project-dependent. These reports are usually required in the first few months after settlement (unless you have negotiated a due diligence clause or secured the property under an option agreement).
- **Air quality engineers** specialise in either indoor or outdoor air quality and work on issues such as emission control, contaminant removal and workplace ventilation. They can be required to design HVAC (heating, ventilation and air conditioning) systems, which are increasing in popularity in passive houses, for example (see chapter 18 for more on passive housing).
- **Civil engineers** will confirm earthworks, levels for slabs, services, stormwater and sewer, and so on. They can't start until the architect has provided the drawings, and so their work is especially time critical.
- **Electrical engineers** design lighting.

- **Environmental engineers** provide guidance on the development's potential environmental impacts. These can include impacts to flora, fauna and waterways. These reports are critical as some sites may have a protected species on the land, which could prevent development altogether. Environmental reports are more common for larger subdivisions on the outskirts of cities, where, for example, native grasses, flora and fauna might need to be inspected. It is recommended to have this report completed as early as possible, as it can make or break a project.

- **Fire engineers** are required for apartment blocks to design firefighting equipment, pumps and fire walls, and so on.

- **Geotechnical engineers** assess the foundations of your proposed development to determine any effect on the foundation design. Geotechnical reports will be more substantial reports if the block is on a slope, has uncontrolled fill or could undermine neighbouring properties. If you were completing a basement dig, for example, a geotechnical engineer would need to provide an assessment on the stability of the excavation and any permanent stability requirements such as soil nails, sheet piling or benching and battering. Once the architect has put together their initial proposal, the geotechnical engineer will provide their expert opinion where required.

- **Hydraulic engineers** design anything to do with water, such as rain collected on the roof and how it's transferred from gutters to downpipes to stormwater. They work in conjunction with civil engineers.

- **Mechanical engineers** deal with ventilation to design extraction units, particularly with basements or internal bathrooms, where they need to design a path for ventilation.

- **Structural engineers** assist with the drawing works and sketch plans to ensure the stability of the structure. Any driveways, retaining walls, slabs, thickening beams, frames, bracing and roofing requires structural engineering input.
- **Traffic engineers** determine turning circles for vehicles and how vehicles will move through the site. This can also include waste removal or service vehicles. This step follows the architect's concept plans.

Landscape architect

The landscape architect assesses the green space required for the project and what planting will be required. They will recommend certain species of plants or grasses best suited for the site depending on the location and where they would be situated within the development, based on factors such as how much shade there is, direct sunlight, and proximity to features such as powerlines and neighbouring properties. They're engaged once the architect has finalised their initial concept.

Arborist

The arborist provides guidance on trees and plants. Some species of trees and plants are endangered and will be protected, and council will want very minimal disruption to them. Other non-native trees and plants, or trees and plants that are dying, dead or dangerous, may be able to be removed as part of the development (and you will also need to factor in fees for the removal of these trees or plants). Arborists' fees will be highly project-dependent.

Quantity surveyor

A quantity surveyor (QS) advises developers on the costs of the total development. They handle a lot of the accounting work produced by the project, including assessing the costs of the designs, administering the building contract tender, advising on the appropriate form of building contract, monitoring the construction and approving stage payments to the contractors. A great QS will also present the developer with cost-effective alternatives to what the architect or builder has proposed.

A QS will provide a report to value the total costs to be paid throughout the construction. This will form a basis for when progress claims will be made and funds drawn down to pay for the works.

Interior designer

Interior design has the power to transform homes by carefully curating the way they look, function and feel. It creates personalised and inspiring spaces that bring comfort and joy to those who live in them. Typically, interior design professionals are expensive, but they can be very beneficial, as interior designers can also assist with selection appointments, interior elevations and internal specifications.

They will help you with 'staging' the development, as staged dwellings often sell faster and for more than empty counterparts. In some cases, the entire staging process is outsourced to a specialised interiors company, but it might simply involve redecorating and rearranging things. The goal is to create an emotional connection with potential buyers rather than having them walk into an empty shell.

Interior design is usually completed in conjunction with the architect finalising construction documentation, particularly when it comes to interior elevations (e.g. bench heights, window heights, niches in bathrooms, door handles, etc.).

The selection appointments such as kitchen, bathroom, tiling, paint and window treatments can be completed during the construction phase.

Development permit

Once you have the basic details of your plan from an engineering and concept perspective, you'll need to submit your application to council, along with any reports to support your application. The council will assess whether to grant you a permit for your development. You'll need to pay a development application fee, and you can submit your application once you have the architectural concept and supporting documents and reports. Your architect or town planner will often complete this application for you.

Project manager

A project manager will manage the entire project. Their role is to speak with consultants, builders, town planners and so on, and ultimately keep track of the project with regard to time and money.

Sometimes, developers play the role of the project manager themselves as a way to save some cash (hello, *Grand Designs*), but this decision should depend on the complexity of the development – it is usually best left to the professionals.

Your project manager is employed to manage the 'team' and the building contract. On your behalf, they supervise the construction and works, as well as executing the building contract and handling the financials (including preparing cash flows, claims handling and payments). Finally, they organise the completion and transfer of as-built files to the owner.

Project managers might charge a flat fee, a profit share or a combination of both, and can be hired at any stage. The earlier the better, though. Read more about project management in Part V.

Building permit / construction certificate

The building permit application can commence once the development permit has been issued. This is when the architect or building designer provides further detailed information regarding the plans. This information can also be referred to as the construction documentation, and this is what prospective builders will refer to when providing quotes and, eventually, during construction. Once the plans are finalised on the back of engineering input, a building certifier will then confirm that all of these requirements have been met according to the relevant standards and council requirements, and if acceptable, they will stamp the plans, which are then able to be used for construction.

The steps that are involved at this stage include but are not limited to the following:

- **Demolition permit.** If there is any existing dwelling on the site, a demolition permit will need to be obtained. If you're relocating the building, a relocation permit may also be required. Once the development permit has been issued, the demolition permit will be the next step. You must have these permits in place before you proceed with demolition, because if somehow you demolish the building before development is approved, you'll be left with a vacant block of land and no income.

- **Energy efficiency report.** A Building Sustainability Index (BASIX) and/or Nationwide House Energy Rating Scheme (NatHERS) energy assessment is conducted to assess the building's energy efficiency and sustainability. Additionally, a statement of environmental effects is typically prepared by the architect, although in certain cases, the expertise of a consulting planner may be sought for specific situations. Each assesses different energy criteria: BASIX looks at water use, energy efficiency and thermal comfort, whereas NatHERS looks purely at a building's thermal performance, providing a star rating on energy needs for heating and cooling.

- **Plumbing and drainage application fee.** Once the design is finalised for plumbing and drainage, an application fee will be made to the relevant authority for connection or 'tap in'.

Certifier

A certifier is generally a qualified building surveyor who can issue building permits or development certificates for building works to commence and carry out inspections on completed works. Certifiers are independent regulators of development and are required to uphold public interest. A principal certifier will carry out mandatory inspections during construction to verify work complies with the development consent and legislative requirements. In the event that a non-compliance is brought to their attention, they will issue a written direction to the developer or builder to verify compliance; if non-compliance continues, they will refer the matter to council.

Organising your finance

Of course, the finance involved in property development is vital. You'll need to secure finance to get any project off the ground, and before, during and over the life of your loan, development and finance structure, you'll be charged a number of fees. It's important to be aware of these so that you factor in ongoing costs. These fees typically include the following:

- **Loan interest.** The lender will charge a nominal interest rate over the course of the construction, which can vary and range from 8 to 12 per cent in the current market. Generally, the interest will be capitalised on the loan.
- **Establishment fee.** This is charged by the lender once the loan is set up. It can vary but is typically up to 3 per cent of the loan amount.
- **Line fee.** This is a fee that a lender can charge to keep the credit or loan available for you to use. Not all lenders will charge this, so ensure that you're including all of these other fees and charges to get an apples-for-apples comparison when reviewing lending options.
- **Brokerage fee.** This is often 1 or 2 per cent of the loan amount and is charged for obtaining your loan.
- **Valuation fee.** The lender will arrange for a valuation to be completed before granting finance approval. This will verify

that the feasibility is within their market analysis in terms of projected margin on the development.

- **Quantity survey progress claim reports.** As each stage of the project is completed, a QS will review the works completed and verify that the progress claim can be completed. These stages include slab, upper frame, roof, lock-up, internal linings, tiling and practical completion.

Building your development

This is the second BIGFIG. During this detailed feasibility stage, you're looking at what the builder will charge to construct what you have designed and plan to develop. Generally, a minimum 5 per cent risk for the construction costs should be added to the feasibility; this will allow for any unknowns during the building process and subsequent variations from the builder.

Choosing a builder

Your builder will be responsible for the physical construction of the development, so be wary about looking for the cheapest possible price – as with most things, you get what you pay for! Instead, aim to pay your builder a reasonable profit in exchange for cost-effective timing and high-performing quality. A builder's financial profit is related to the building's cost and the length of contract.

Builders with the right experience may also be able to take on the role of management contractor, managing the various subcontractors for the developer in return for a fee. Subcontractors will handle specialist responsibilities out of the scope of what is possible for the builder.

There are two options for obtaining pricing from potential builders:

1. **Design and construct** (D&C) begins early, when a builder becomes involved during the design phase. Your aim is

to leverage the builder's time and expertise to optimise your design and increase constructability. Builders will also recommend their preferred structural engineers and consultants – usually those they've worked with before and trust – to make sure construction costs stay down.

2. **Documented tender** is where you work with the architect to coordinate the design and finalise the package. This is then sent out to potential builders. This is the more popular option.

It's extremely important that the build contract details what is included and excluded in the price. This ensures that you compare like for like when you're considering quotes from builders, because often they'll price the project differently. For example, some builders may exclude certain items that others include, or have 'provisional sum' items that aren't necessarily included in the initial price but then have rates or lump sums detailed if those specified items arise during construction. The more detail you can include in the earlier development and building permit phases, the better, as this leaves less assumptions to the builder.

Demolition

If there is an existing dwelling on the site, you will need to factor in demolition costs. As part of the demolition process, you'll need to take care of a few things:

- **Disconnecting the electricity.** You'll need to organise this with the approval of the local power authority.

- **Dilapidation report.** This provides details on the condition of the asset, as well as any defects if there is any potential impact on neighbouring properties or nearby infrastructure, such as roads, kerbs, gutters and fences. This protects you from having to pay for these after your development's completion.

Inspections during construction

Once construction has commenced, there can be other inspections and works to be completed outside of the build contract:

- **Engineering inspections.** These will be sporadic, with sign-off required for all major structural engineering works, such as inspection of foundations prior to pouring the slab and installing structural steel components.
- **External works.** This is a broad category that covers off anything outside the physical site required to facilitate the development, such as upgrading stormwater networks or roads, installing kerbs and gutters, and adding in extra crossovers.
- **Plumbing and drainage.** These must be inspected to verify they have been installed and connected to existing infrastructure correctly.
- **Sewer pump.** These are required if you need to pump sewerage from a lower level up to the street, for example. It's critical that anything to do with sewerage is identified in the earlier feasibility, because it can be costly, challenging and time consuming if you need to address these services later. It can sometimes kill the deal if you physically can't connect the service due to access restrictions or lack of a nearby connection.

Don't expect that once you have engaged a builder there will be no issues. You'll see in our case studies at the back of the book how quickly and unexpectedly things can pop up or go wrong.

Post-construction connections

Upon construction completion, you'll require the following connections:

- **Electricity.** Once all civil and building works are completed, the local power authority will connect the power. You may need an electrical transformer to upgrade the power to the site, too, if you're adding extra dwellings. This will need to be completed by an electrical contractor prior to the power being supplied to the new building/s (towards the end of the construction phase). A word of advice: these companies move notoriously slowly, so the more time you give to ensuring the works are completed to the correct standard at this step, the better, and the faster you will be able to sell the development.

- **Gas.** A fee will be charged by the local authority to direct gas to the property and to make additional connections required for new dwellings.

- **Sewer.** If there are additional sewer connections to be made, the local authority will charge a fee for the connection.

- **Water.** If there are additional water connections to be made, the local authority will charge a fee for the connection.

For gas, sewer and water connections, the fee will include an application charge and any new infrastructure charges.

Holding costs and income

When it comes to holding your property, there are costs involved and potentially incomes received.

Just like holding a residential or commercial property, there are a number of bills you'll need to pay:

- **Council rates** will be charged to you, as the owner, quarterly throughout your development.

- **Public liability insurance** will protect you against third-party damage or injury.

- **Building insurance** will protect you against property damage due to a damage or acts of God.

- **Land tax** may be applicable depending on how the project is structured and the value of the land. It will be charged over the duration of the project.

- **Water and sewerage rates,** similar to council rates, will be charged quarterly for usage and supply.

Some of these will only apply until you obtain your development approval, such as the insurances and utilities; once the building is demolished and services disconnected, you won't be paying these anymore.

You may decide to rent the property out for 6 to 12 months if there are predicted delays with council, for example. This will ensure income is coming in to help with the holding costs. If the property is leased after settlement, just like with an investment property, you'll receive this additional income until the property becomes vacant. For developments, the vacancy will come when you're ready to commence and demolish the property to enable construction. If the existing lease has a fixed term, you'll need to keep this in mind regarding the timing of the development.

Registering your titles

Once you complete the development, you might strata-title the properties before selling them off. In that case, you'll need to establish a body corporate. The body corporate will ultimately be responsible for managing the complex, obtaining and maintaining insurance policies, collecting administration and sinking fund contributions from owners or tenants, and maintaining common property. As the developer, you'll be responsible for appointing and then establishing the body corporate, which will need to be sorted out prior to settlement. This information needs to be provided on the disclosure statement, which forms part of the sales documentation.

This stage includes several key steps:

- **Infrastructure contributions.** Every council has infrastructure contributions, which you as the developer will need to pay as part of the approval documentation. These fees cover the maintenance of additional services required, such as stormwater, community facilities, road networks, parks and footpaths. They're charged when the development receives approval.

- **Body corporate establishment.** Prior to settlement, if you plan to strata-title the development, you'll need to appoint and establish a Body Corporate Manager. It can vary across states and territories, but their general role is to undertake functions required under body corporate legislation and administer common property and body corporate assets for the benefits of all owners.

- **Insurance.** You'll need to take out insurance to cover the new buildings and any liabilities after construction is complete. The builder will generally hold this insurance under their own insurance during construction and, once practical completion is achieved, this risk will be passed over to the developer before the units are sold. You need to ensure the builder's insurance is valid and up to date; there are additional insurances you can obtain to cover you for this. You can engage an 'insurance broker' who specialises in getting the correct and most adequate insurance for your needs. They typically only charge a small administration fee and get the bulk of their fee through the insurer (similar to a mortgage broker). Note that if a body corporate needs to be established, the building insurance will need to be transferred to that entity prior to settlement.

- **Plan sealing.** You'll need to pay the plan sealing application fee with council, which confirms that construction has finished. It sets you up to receive your titles.

- **Survey plan.** The surveyor will create a survey plan, which is a legal and technical document outlining the details of the new property's dimensions and boundaries. It's required for establishing new land titles, easements or covenants.

Once these steps have been taken, along with connecting and signing off on all utilities, paying all costs and contributions, and meeting all development conditions, you can apply for your title registration. This means you can then move to your next stage.

Marketing and selling your development

The marketing stage is a critical part of the sales process. There will be several steps involved when you reach this point, which you'll need to determine with your development sales agent.

Your first consideration is advertising and how the property will be marketed. This includes preparing brochures, listing online, taking photos and preparing renders, and so on. You'll need to work out whether you market and advertise early 'off the plan' or wait until nearer to project completion. The timing can be early to facilitate pre-sales, mid-construction to secure off-the-plan commitments, or nearer to project completion.

These will be your main considerations at this point:

- **Agent fees.** Your sales agent will assist you in the marketing and sales process. They will help with negotiations, arranging contracts, preparing sales advice and so on, and will charge a commission based on the sale price, which is generally 1.5 to 3 per cent. Additional costs for marketing may also be charged on top of the commission.

- **Conveyancing.** A conveyancer will assist in the sales process when it comes to contract exchange and title transfer at settlement. They should be engaged prior to marketing to prepare the contract document.

- **Off-the-plan contracts.** If you decide to sell off the plan, you'll need to prepare off-the-plan contracts. These will be completed by a solicitor.

- **Staging.** Staging is about presenting a completed property to allow potential buyers to visualise how it would look fully furnished.

Making your money

This is the third of the BIGFIGs – what the end product will sell for. Ensure you canvass multiple opinions from different agents in the area to get a good understanding of what your finished development will likely sell for. If you shoot too high, you can make a potential development site look better than it is. If you are too conservative, you could pass on a site with a great opportunity.

It's also important to understand the projected gross realisation value (GRV) for the development. This is what the bank will use to determine how financially viable the project is. As a developer, you can use this to assess how much potential equity you'll have on completion if you decide to hold onto the completed stock. When it comes to cash flow, you'll effectively be holding an asset at cost price but returning market rent, which can be extremely lucrative!

As each unit is sold and settled, the proceeds will be received by the developer. Once revenue is derived from the sales, revenue will generally be distributed in the following order:

1. External debt to any lenders will be paid off.
2. The development management fee will be paid.
3. Any loan partners will be reimbursed.
4. The developer will be reimbursed for any development costs.
5. Profits over and above will be paid to the developer.

Sensitivity analysis

As a developer, you can prepare a feasibility analysis around the current market, but you can't predict where the market will be at completion. That's why, as part of your due diligence, you should also include a sensitivity analysis of some of these key figures, such as land acquisition, build cost, finance, interest rates and sale prices, because these can all go up or down at any given time.

Put simply, a sensitivity analysis is an economic projection that prepares for a range of assumptions, including the downside or upside of the project, to address the risk of a different outcome from the one expected in your feasibility. A sensitivity analysis protects you from market changes such as rental rates, sales prices, interest rates, operating expenses and development costs. In a growing market, you could expect on completion that the sale prices will be more than today's value, but do not rely on this to make profit.

The sensitivity analysis is performed using spreadsheets and is easily adjustable to factor in the percentage changes under each item.

CHAPTER SEVEN
BUILDING YOUR FOUNDATION TEAM

A key difference between purchasing property to live in or invest in and buying property to develop is that you'll need more people in your team. As in the first two books in this series, development isn't something you can or should do solo; you'll need to bring together a 'foundation' team of trusted individuals to assist you through the process.

The list of people you'll need on your team is long. That's because there are more layers to development than residential or commercial investing. You're not simply facilitating the sale of a property but bringing bricks and mortar to life, and then managing it when it's built.

There are multiple ways to find the members of your foundation team, with referrals and online searches being the most common. However, one of the best methods is to find successful investors and developers and ask them who they use. Very successful investors and developers have strong teams they can trust. The members of your team must be very experienced in developments, not just buying and selling investment properties as in standard residential acquisitions.

You'll come to rely on these people when making the strategic decisions in the active part of your development, which means they will come in and out at different times during the process. You'll also need to rely on a whole bunch of other specialists, consultants and professionals, and we covered the full list of those in chapter 6.

Finally, there's a running order of when you'll need to engage each member in your team. With more people involved, you need to know at what point each person needs to be involved. Many of these foundation team members you will have already engaged as part of the detailed feasibility, as we discussed their roles in the previous chapter, but let's look at the remaining foundation advisers in general order of acquisition, what they do and why you may need them.

Also, try not to focus on the cost of engaging each of these experts. They can all make or break your development, so go with the best for your needs, not the cheapest!

Accountant

Your accountant will ensure everything to do with the financing is structured properly. Trust us, you need an accountant who specialises in property, and preferably with experience in development, as opposed to a general business accountant. They will guide you on the tax implications of the development and GST regulations, and play a huge role in helping you structure the development based on whether you plan to sell or hold the completed project. They will be a constant presence through the life cycle of the development, so it's important to choose your accountant wisely!

Mortgage broker

A development mortgage broker is your middleperson with financial institutions, such as banks, non-banks and private lenders.

They will scan several lenders to secure you the most suitable loan (with regard to both interest rates and terms).

It's important to note that brokers often come at no cost to you, because they're providing the lender with a customer and are subsequently paid by the lender.

Great brokers will understand your needs and help manage your best interests, and when you're ready will present the lender's guidelines to your servicing or development potential. The lender will ensure that the proposed development is viable and well located (for the market demographic), as well as assessing whether the developer has the ability to complete the project. As development finance incurs more risk, lenders require larger deposits (as security) than for typical residential property purchases, and lenders may also ask for property itself as security.

Solicitor

Solicitors are vital to the development process when it comes to contracts and settlements. They're your insurance to avoid mistakes through the process of the various transactions within a development, and they will also help you with your funding arrangements from start to finish.

Typically, you'll engage a solicitor upfront when you're looking to acquire a site, then you'll engage them later when it comes time to sell. It's worth noting that some solicitors are only licensed to practise in particular states or territories.

Property lawyer

A property lawyer can become involved in more technical projects where you might require an option agreement, a development management agreement or other legal documentation drafted to facilitate the development and protect yours and the seller's rights.

Read more about the role of solicitors and property lawyers in chapter 8.

Real estate agent

Agents are an important part of the game. They'll be the middle-person who will help you negotiate with the landowner (seller) and can advise you on matters relating to the assessment stage. If they're used well, they'll help you to find sites with development potential, as well as helping you extract the most value from the deal when it comes time to sell.

Generally, agents have a strong understanding of the market, and will be able to advise you on what certain properties are worth and who is likely to buy those properties.

In practice, agents walk the seller and the buyer through the process of the transaction and are compensated by the seller in the form of a percentage-based fee at the end of the deal when the transaction is successful. Note that the agent who sold you the development site may not be the best agent to sell the completed product.

Buyer's agent

You'll need to decide whether you have the time to search for and negotiate the site acquisition. If you're struggling to find a site, you can always engage a buyer's agent. They can enable you to access off-market opportunities you wouldn't normally get access to. A good buyer's agent who specialises in sourcing development sites will also have a thorough understanding of what sites will potentially stack up. They will also potentially be able to negotiate the purchase price down further, ultimately saving you time and money. Their fee for service can vary but is generally around 2 per cent of the acquisition price.

Development management

Not all projects will require it, but you have the option to engage a development manager if the project can afford it and you can benefit from it. A development manager takes on an overarching role across your whole project. They will take on the project management part (or could appoint a third party or utilise services similiar to those offered by Palise Property – see part V) as well as the initial acquisition and approval phases.

The main role of the development manager is to optimise the project and understand the **highest and best use** for the site (as discussed in chapter 5). Once this is determined, the development manager will assist with site acquisition and arranging consultants for design, town planning and surveying to move ahead with the development application and approval. Once this is obtained, the development manager will proceed with project feasibility and financing, construction tender selection and appointment, project budget and cash flow, sales and marketing, and all legal requirements.

The process of a property development and the sequence of steps are critical knowledge that a good development manager will understand. They will be highly experienced in making educated decisions that will impact the project to be delivered on budget, on time and to the agreed standards.

Depending on the size of the project, a development manager may appoint a project manager to administer the construction contract. This is more common in large-scale projects.

Development management and project management fees can vary, again depending on the size of the project, and they can be a fixed fee or a profit-split percentage. For standard duplex or townhouse projects, the project management fee could be anywhere from $60,000 to $100,000, depending on the complexity and profitability of the project. Development managers can cost a minimum of

20 per cent of the profit split, which again will vary depending on the level of involvement and complexity of the project.

**

When vetting potential members of your foundation team, look at their qualifications, of course, but also consider the following questions:

- Do you like them? This is very important, as is the reverse, because if they like you, they're more likely to work hard for you.
- Do they sound competent and confident? Check out their website and reviews.
- What is their experience? Have they been in the business long? Do they have the skillset for your particular development?
- Do you feel you can trust them? Assess what personal benefit they'll get from your business.
- Do they have good communication skills, and do you feel they'll deliver when they say they will?
- Do they fit your risk temperament? Ask questions about their own appetite for risk and see how closely this aligns with yours.
- Do you fundamentally agree with their property thesis? You have to be confident in what they're doing and the way they perform.

If you can, try to speak with their previous clients; they'll usually be happy to share their views. It's important to understand how the consultant differs to their competitors. You can ask them to provide the details of some previous clients to discuss this with.

Any one member of your foundation team is worth their fees many times over. A mentor of some kind (paid or unpaid) can also be invaluable.

PART IV
CONVEYANCING, FINANCE AND BUYING STRUCTURES

You've done the hard work on your due diligence and analysed and assessed the most important details. But that's only part of the process. Now, let's look at the legal and financial aspects of property purchases. Conveyancing, choosing and obtaining finance, and deciding on the right ownership structure for your investments all require careful consideration if you're to achieve the best possible investment outcome. While the process is similar to buying a 'typical' residential or commercial property, development projects have additional complex layers. Let's take a look.

CHAPTER EIGHT
CONVEYANCING

The main purpose of the conveyancing process is to transfer the legal title or ownership of the property from one party to another. The process usually starts from the time you enter into your contract (the date of the contract) and continues through to the settlement of the purchase. The conveyancing work is performed by a solicitor or conveyancer: a solicitor is a legally trained professional, while a conveyancer has been taught conveyancing but isn't trained in law.

The solicitor or conveyancer you choose needs to be well versed in the laws of the state or territory in which they work, as there are many differences between the states and territories. Look for someone who's highly experienced in developments, not just the person with the cheapest rates. The settlements of a development process can be messy, so you need someone who's confident in what they do and will have your best interests at heart.

What you need to know

The steps of the conveyancing process are fairly similar for each development, but understanding the specific elements that you'll need for your development early on can make the difference between success and failure. A good conveyancer will help you understand the physical details, such as the right zoning if you're developing on a lot, building restrictions, sewer diagrams and soil testing.

A good conveyancer will also school you on the great unknown. You don't know what you don't know, and if you aren't aware of an issue to do with your lot then it'll only bite you later. Remember that different information will probably change the outcome and the cost.

Finally, a good conveyancer will also advise you to have a financial buffer to account for the unknown. As we've said before, developing is not for the faint-hearted, so if you can protect yourself by having some capital in your back pocket, you'll be in the best position possible to weather some of the storms. Every day you're developing your site, you're paying holding costs, which can be thousands of dollars. Even small developments incur holding costs, such as interest, council rates, land tax and services, so it pays to set everything up correctly in the beginning.

For example, it pays to do your due diligence with all the contingencies. If you know that there are big changes to come in with council regulations, make sure you protect yourself by understanding what's happening. You might avoid what happened to one couple who bought land to build a double-storey duplex, had the plans drawn up and engineering sorted, and were ready to go. When the council changed its regulations regarding minimum lot sizes, suddenly their development couldn't go ahead as planned, and they could only build single-storey dwellings. They had to scramble around for finance, redo the plans and then reduce the sale price due to the smaller configuration, losing out across the board.

Conveyancing horror story

One of our recommended conveyancers had a client a few years ago who came to them and said that he'd bought a lot and was building a duplex. The plan was to sell them off. Nothing wrong with that, but it was clear from the get-go that he didn't know what he was doing. When he was asked who was building the development, he said he had a builder. Then, when he was asked who was subdividing the land, he said the builder was. When he was told that the builder doesn't look after the subdivision, that this was done by a surveyor, he looked blank. The conveyancer asked him, 'Where's your surveyor?' He replied that he didn't know and that the builder was organising it. So, the conveyancer went back to the builder and asked him who was organising the subdivision, and he said he didn't know and that he had only been engaged to build.

Because this client had already engaged his builder, and with the build likely to take about nine months, he was fast losing money. He'd jumped in head-first, and didn't understand the importance of taking the right steps and engaging professionals early. In the end, the conveyancer helped him find a surveyor so he could subdivide the land, and he did finish the build, but he admitted that the duplex nearly led him to bankruptcy and he lost a lot of money. In the end, he simply wanted the development finished as quickly as possible because it was sending him into the ground. He learnt some painful lessons in the process.

How a conveyancer works

Conveyancers are usually engaged from the start to help you with your due diligence. They typically charge a one-off fee, and their initial engagement might be for anywhere between 8 and 12 weeks, depending on the development. After they give their initial advice, there may be more work for them to do at certain points, such as when you're developing the land, getting the build ready and then preparing to start selling off the plan.

They typically charge in set phases, depending on what you need. If you're looking at buying a lot, the conveyancing cost will be a set purchase, but then if you're looking to sell a block of two townhouses, for example, the conveyancer will charge per sale.

As we mentioned before, the conveyancing process differs depending on your state or territory but, basically, once you and the seller have agreed on all the terms of the contract and signed it, the contract will be dated on the date the last person signed. This is known as 'exchanging contracts' or the property being 'under contract'. The contract is legally binding after it's been signed by both parties. The deposit is usually paid before the buyer signs, but in some states and territories it can be done after signing, as specified in the contract. The amount of deposit is negotiated between the parties through the sales agent and is paid to the agent as the stakeholder, either on signing or on another date as agreed between the parties.

The contract will contain conditions that the buyer needs to satisfy, including due diligence, finance approval and the various testing, building, engineering and other consultancy requirements. During the period between the signing of the contract and satisfaction of these clauses, the contract is known as 'conditional'; once the clauses are satisfied, the contract becomes 'unconditional', and the buyer and seller must proceed to settlement.

During the due diligence period, your solicitor or conveyancer will undertake pre-purchase searches and enquiries. These include checks with government and non-government authorities to ensure there are no outstanding interests or problems with the property. Some of these searches can be performed after the contract is unconditional if they will not affect the outcome of the sale.

The list of searches that can be undertaken is extensive, so it's best to discuss with your solicitor or conveyancer which are appropriate for your transaction, because the costs to carry out these searches can add up quickly. The most common are:

- title search
- registered plan

- local authority rates
- special water-meter reading
- land tax
- transport and main roads
- priority notice.

Your solicitor or conveyancer can arrange an inspection of the body corporate records (also known as a strata report), but many other companies can also do this work. This report needs to be obtained and reviewed before going unconditional on a contract.

Once the contract becomes unconditional, a settlement date is booked with all parties (including any outgoing or incoming lenders). Before settlement day, any special conditions – such as repairs or removal of items left at the property – must be satisfied; this is usually checked through a pre-settlement inspection.

For settlement to occur, all parties, including the lenders, must be ready to settle. Transfer documents must be signed and returned, and stamp duty paid if it's a paper settlement, or all matters completed on PEXA, the e-conveyance platform for Property Exchange Australia. The parties' respective solicitors or conveyancers will prepare the transfer documents, arrange for the seller to organise the release of the mortgage (if there is one) and liaise with the banks to prepare for settlement.

Before settlement, the solicitors or conveyancers will ensure all documents have been prepared and executed correctly, settlement figures have been adjusted accurately and everything necessary has been completed.

On settlement day, the parties' solicitors or conveyancers and their lender representatives will be present for the buyer to pay the balance of the purchase price in exchange for the title transfer and release of the mortgage. If the seller has a mortgage, the seller will give their lender's representative a cheque (or certified electronic transfer) to pay out this mortgage in exchange for its release.

After settlement, the solicitor or conveyancer will contact the seller's real estate agent, authorising the release of the keys to the buyer and the deposit to the seller.

If the buyer has obtained finance from a lender, the lender will attend to the registration of the transfer, the release of mortgage (if any) and registration of the buyer's mortgage with the land registry services. If the property is being bought with cash, the buyer's solicitor will attend to the registration of the requisite documents. If the transaction was performed through PEXA, payment of the purchase price and registration of the transfer, release of the seller's mortgage and registration of the buyer's mortgage will occur immediately online.

Once settlement has occurred, the buyer becomes the legal owner of the property, and the seller is released from any further obligations for payment of rates or taxes – these become the buyer's responsibility. The lender will usually hold the title of the property until the loan is paid off.

Conveyancers versus property lawyers

While a conveyancer manages the legalities of your potential development site, a property lawyer is needed for anything outside of the property, such as statutes and bylaws involved in larger unit and multi-apartment blocks.

As with conveyancers, every state and territory has different property laws practised by different service professionals. For example, in Western Australia there are only settlement agents, while in Queensland you need to be a lawyer or employed by a law firm to do any conveyancing work.

Our tip is to find a lawyer or conveyancer who has experience in what you're proposing, as they do range widely in expertise. Some specialise in mum-and-dad development purchases, while others deal more with commercial purchasers or small duplexes.

A good rule of thumb is to engage your conveyancer or property lawyer before you sign anything. It's an obvious step, but by doing so, your lawyer can advise you on some of the finer points, such as how you'll secure the property or the best conditions to introduce option agreements. There are many different ways to structure a contract, depending on you, your goals and your development, and a good property lawyer will guide you through these so you aren't caught short, like the client from the conveyancing horror story we shared earlier.

Our best advice is to hire carefully – trust recommendations and lock your conveyancer or property lawyer in early.

Options and conditions

A property lawyer will be able to use options and conditions in your contract as a way to mitigate risks along the way, and to either sell or buy in the future for a particular price. An option agreement will sit in front of your contract and place certain agreements on buying and selling the property. There are two types of option agreements: a 'call' option and a 'put' option.

The call option is granted by the owner, giving the buyer the right, but not the obligation, to **buy** that property. In other words, it means that you're not locked in to buy the property but you have the right to it, giving you time to do due diligence or finalise other terms. If things don't stack up for whatever reason, you can just walk away without too much of a financial hit. Call options are common in property developments and usually last six to 12 months. On the other hand, a put option gives the buyer the right, but not the obligation, to **sell** the property to a buyer they line up before the option expires. There are also 'put and call' options, which go both ways. A good property lawyer will be able to advise you on the best option if relevant.

Property lawyer horror story

Before COVID-19, one of our clients bought a site and had plans to develop it into a 45-apartment building. During construction, the costs went through the roof – it was going to cost him more to build these apartments than he expected to receive from the sale proceeds – but he was locked in.

He was operating at a loss and was nowhere near finishing and, as the developer, he still needed to seem to be actively progressing the development. There was a clause in the contract that stated if the development became commercially unviable – which it was – then the developer could terminate the contracts, but this would upset all the buyers, who had taken action to sell their homes and wanted to move in, so the developer didn't want to terminate.

The solution was to increase the price for the buyers, which meant the developer could cover the additional construction costs, and the buyers were still ahead because the market value of the property had gone up significantly more than they had paid for it. Most of the buyers agreed to pay extra because they were still getting a good deal, and those properties whose buyers decided to walk away were resold by the developer for a higher amount.

The moral of the story is this: first, try to buy under market value so that you can increase the price to cover construction costs if you need to and, second, lock in the construction costs as much as possible, as that would have allowed the developer to avoid this situation entirely.

Setting up for success

The most successful developers have a rinse-and-repeat system: they get the right advice and the right structure and simply repeat it again and again. For those with no runs on the board, it can be hard to get set up, because most developers don't make a lot of money on their first development and good lawyers aren't cheap. However, a development that goes belly up midway is more expensive!

As you saw in chapter 6, if you know your numbers, have kept things simple and have your team behind you, you'll set yourself up for success from the beginning.

CHAPTER NINE
TYPES OF LENDERS AND LOANS

Development property loans are transacted similarly to residential property loans by the major banks, but there are other options available, and they can differ dramatically in the way they operate. You can find more in-depth information on this in Steve's previous books, but let's summarise here and then show you how development lenders and loans differ.

Types of lenders

Let's take a closer look at the different types of lenders:

- **Major banks** are the most common type of lender and the type most people are familiar with. Banks are generally owned by shareholders and are usually listed on the stock exchange.

- **Mutuals** are building societies and credit unions; they're owned by members, not shareholders. They're authorised deposit-taking institutions and are regulated by the Australian Prudential Regulation Authority (APRA) to the same extent that banks are.

- **Private funders** (or lenders) are often a conglomerate of wealthy people who pool their money to lend funds at premium rates. They generally charge high interest rates and establishment fees, are more focused on security than your ability to service the loan, and are more interested in the quality of the property and tenant when determining the loan amount. It can be a lot easier and faster to obtain loans from private lenders, too, because their loans are not covered by the *National Consumer Credit Protection Act 2009*.

How development lenders differ

More and more, we're seeing developers use non-banks for lending rather than the Big Four. A non-bank lender is a lender that doesn't hold a banking licence – they use their own money and usually come in the form of a building society or credit union. A lot of people assume that smaller lenders will not be as safe as the big banks; however, all financial institutions in Australia are regulated by independent government bodies, so smaller lenders are just as safe.

Non-bank lenders provide several benefits. Their competitive rates mean they can provide solutions for borrowers who don't meet standard bank lending criteria (such as if they've maxed out their borrowing cap). Some non-banks can lend up to nine times your income, compared to six times from a bank.

Here are some key questions to ask your potential financier:

- Would you lend on this type of project?
- What are your lending limits?
- Do you lend towards total development cost (TDC) or just hard costs (i.e. direct build costs **only**, excluding indirect costs such as consultants, legal fees, insurance, interest, etc.)?
- Do you lend towards GST?
- Do you capitalise the interest?
- What is your current pre-sale policy?

- Do you lend on a limited or non-recourse basis, i.e. if the borrower defaults the lender can seize the collateral (property) but they cannot seek any further compensation? (If so, under what circumstances?)
- What is your current pricing (line fees, margins, establishment fees)?
- Do you charge a commitment fee (similar to a line fee, but charged annually)?
- Do you charge loan extension/rollover fees?
- Do you charge early repayment fees?
- How do you treat developers retaining completed property?
- Who is on your quantity surveyor (QS) and valuer panel?
- Do you allow the developer to engage the QS and valuer?

Types of loans

It's crucial you choose the right loan type for your development. Most residential loans are over 20 to 30 years and are either principal and interest (P&I) or interest only (IO). IO loans are capped at five years. If you're developing, you should already know the difference (or perhaps you're in the wrong game!), but let's recap and then show you how different loan types impact developments.

- **Fixed versus variable interest rate loans.** Fixed rates enable you to lock in your interest rate (and therefore your loan repayments) for a set period, usually one to five years. Variable rates are more flexible: loans with variable rates generally allow you to make extra repayments, and also to redraw on the repayments. Extracting equity to grow your portfolio is possible under variable loans but not fixed loans.
- **Principal-and-interest versus interest-only loans.** P&I loans are the most common type for everyday investors, but IO loans are

more popular for residential property investors as they're tax-effective and will increase a portfolio's cash flow due to the lower repayments. No principal is paid off the loan during the loan term (which is usually three to five years), only the interest on the borrowings. Once the loan's term is completed, it will revert to a P&I loan unless the property is refinanced. Some investors opt for IO loans and then deposit any excess cash into their offset account for future deposits or investment opportunities.

- **Full documentation, low documentation and no documentation loans.** The full documentation (or 'full doc') loan is the most common type of mortgage issued by Australian lenders. You'll have to provide more information for this than for any other loan application, including details of your income, asset base, outgoings and debts. Low documentation ('low doc') and no documentation ('no doc') loans require fewer forms of document to qualify for a loan. They were popular before the Global Financial Crisis (GFC) but are now less common.

- **Lines of credit.** A line of credit allows you to use equity from your principal place of residence (PPOR) or investment properties (either commercial or residential). It functions in a similar way to a credit card: you have a pre-approved credit limit and can borrow as much of this as you want, paying interest on the outstanding balance. Note that a line of credit is not amortised – that is, your regular payments don't reduce or pay off the debt.

- **Split loans.** A split loan has two accounts: a fixed-interest portion and a variable-rate portion. You can allocate as much as you want to each account, as long as it's allowed by your lender. This allows you to manage the risk of interest-rate fluctuations but also take advantage if rates drop with the variable component.

How development loans differ

The biggest difference with development loans is that the interest is capitalised – you don't pay it throughout the course of the loan period. The interest is added to the loan, and the lender will draw down from this capitalised interest during the construction. The loan period will be fixed, so you need to be clear on your development timelines. If construction and settlements take longer than expected, you may need to re-apply for finance, which can include another round of application fees, valuations and potentially penalty interest. Sometimes the loan can be extended with a 'rollover fee'. If you manage to finish the development early, there may be an early exit fee.

Another component to understand is how GST is treated and calculated. If the loan doesn't cover GST, you'll need to cover this amount during the construction phase. You can claim the GST back every quarter, so it's wise to allow for two months' worth of GST during construction.

The loan process

Once the contract of sale is signed, it's sent to the broker or lender so they can begin processing your loan. Finance approval is typically the most stressful part of a property purchase. The larger your portfolio, the more complicated the lending and valuation procedure becomes.

If the contract is subject to finance, you'll be trying to obtain finance at the same time as being under contract. It's critical that your mortgage broker and lender have all the information they need from the start of the process, including proof of your personal information and financial history.

The land acquisition phase is processed the same way for a development as for residential property purchasing, but there are a few areas where you can boost your application, which we'll go into in this section.

Your personal information

As outlined in Steve's previous books, as part of your loan application you will need to provide the following information:

- Formal proof of identification (may be required if you haven't borrowed from a particular lender before and includes your passport, driver's licence, birth certificate and government identification cards such as your Medicare card)
- Details about your current address
- The number and ages of any dependants you have (children or otherwise)
- Your relationship status.

Property finance horror story

One of our clients was a first-time developer who got very excited at an auction, bought a property, went unconditional and – big mistake – signed the contract in his own name. He had plans of developing the property straight away because the numbers were strong. He started making good on his plans and made quite a bit of money – before suddenly having to pay 47 per cent tax, the highest marginal tax rate, on the profit. His problem was that he owned the property as an individual; ownership should have been in the name of a company, which would have meant a tax rate of 25 cents to the dollar instead of 47 cents.

By the time we found out, it was too late. We couldn't go back and change it because it would have cost too much. Because he had the wrong ownership structure in place, he had no choice other than to pay the tax. In the end, he lost more than $300,000, which came out of his profit. (More about structures in chapter 11.)

The message is that the business plan of a development is only as good as its structure. Understand the asset you're buying and the business plan around it to utilise the right tax structure, and don't make the same mistake as this developer!

The five Cs of credit

It's also a good idea to consider the 'five Cs of credit': character, capacity, capital, collateral and conditions. Lenders use these to determine the risk associated with a loan.

Here's a summary:

1. **Character** refers to the fact that lenders want to know if you – the borrower – and any guarantors are honest and have integrity, to give them confidence that you have the background, education and stability of employment to pay back the loan. Given that a lender will examine the personal credit of all borrowers and guarantors involved, you need to ensure your past financial information is sound. If you have any delinquencies, be prepared to explain them.

2. **Capacity** means serviceability, or your ability to repay a loan. Lenders base their assessment of your capacity on a number of factors, including your income, the loan amount, your age, and your other commitments and expenses. The bank uses these factors to calculate a debt service ratio (DSR), which is the percentage of your monthly income they expect you will spend on debts. Lenders take into account factors such as overtime, commission, company cars, regular expenses, credit-card debts (and their limits), car loans, student loans, the number of children or dependants living in your home, second jobs and rental income you receive from a property portfolio. These can all negatively affect your loan serviceability and make it much harder to obtain finance. To increase your chances, it's essential to minimise the limits on all credit cards and always pay any personal and car loans on time.

3. **Capital** represents your wealth and any assets or valuables that make up your total net worth. In short, it's the value of your assets minus your liabilities. The lender considers your savings, investments such as real estate and shares, the value of your car and other assets, minus any personal loans and credit card and other debts. Lenders would like to see you have a buffer that would allow you to keep paying your loan if you had a financial setback, such as losing your job. By looking at your capital, lenders assess your ability and willingness to save and accumulate assets, and then compare this with your age.

4. **Collateral** is an important consideration, but its significance varies between different types of loan. Generally, collateral is represented by the properties used to secure the loan. If you can't provide collateral or security in the form of property, some lenders offer guarantor loans, which use a third party's collateral as a backup. If you're cross-collateralising – using another property as security to obtain the loan – and are unable to make the agreed repayments, the bank has the right to seize the property to repay the debt. However, they usually explore all other avenues before they do this, including reducing or freezing the repayments for a period. If the lender does end up selling your property, you retain any capital gains from the sale.

5. **Conditions** refers to the financial conditions at the time you submit your application – specifically your interest rate, principal amount and general market conditions. It encompasses any outside circumstances that may affect your financial situation and ability to make loan repayments. Lenders may evaluate the overall business climate, both within your industry and in associated industries, and the economic conditions that could affect your borrowing, including the Reserve Bank's cash rate and any policy changes that affect

borrowers' ability to borrow money. These factors can affect the lender's allowable LVR on the property.

How the process differs for developments

The lending process is all about making a case for the lender to give you the capital you require, and the good news is there are ways you can improve your chances.

At the end of the day, the lender is assessing whether to give you a loan based on a piece of dirt in a suburb it may never have heard of. If you can make yourself and your proposition look as attractive as possible, this will help you significantly – for example, if you can show that your numbers stack up, and you can show a physical image of what your development will look like once completed. Lenders will also assess your past performance, so you'll need a proven track record or experience. Remember that the way you present your numbers to the bank for assessment is critical.

If you can bypass the retail loan stage, financing can be more straightforward. Going straight to a commercial loan will mean the lender won't be looking into your personal servicing; it's all about how the numbers stack up for the development. How well you can negotiate terms for the land acquisition will determine whether you can skip the retail loan. For example, if you negotiate an option over the site whereby you have six to 12 months to apply for development approval (DA), you can exercise the option once you have the DA and go straight to construction finance.

Valuations

Once the finance application has started, a valuation will be performed. Generally, this is organised by the bank or broker (for a retail development). While a straightforward property valuation is performed in three main ways – a desktop valuation or automated valuation model (AVM), a kerbside valuation or a full valuation – the requirements for a development valuation are higher-level and more complex, especially for commercial developments.

What you need to do

For the valuer to do their job, you'll need to give them a report first. This will include the:

- type of project
- status of the project
- location (proximity to services)
- development team (architect, town planner, engineers)
- timetables (program).

You'll also need to build in pricing from one or two builders. It's important to obtain quotes with turnaround times, because the build cost is fixed depending on timeframes; if it drags out, the build cost may change. You'll need pricing to substantiate your:

- estimate plans (if approved)
- Building approval (BA) and/or development approval (DA) (see chapter 13 for more on these)
- standards of finish
- GST structure (supporting letter from accountant)
- sales information
- marketing material
- feasibility (in valuer's format, i.e. excluding financing costs such as line fees, establishment fees, broker fees, the equity contribution and structuring or buying entity costs).

Then, arrange a time to meet the valuer to go through the report.

What you need to know

We have a few tips to help with this crucial step of your development.

First, you can choose your own valuer rather than relying on the one the bank or lender provides, but they must be on your financier's approved panel.

Second, valuers can do cross-checks on similar sites to ensure your development is comparable and appropriate. This is based on square-metre rates. They will also use market rates when they value your cost inputs, such as pricing for your consultants and agents, so make sure you use fair estimates. Also, assume everything is being sold within your development, and don't include the property management fee or equity contribution.

Finally, if you're building multiple properties, your lender may need the valuer to value your properties 'all in one line', meaning that all properties are included on the one title. If they value each property individually, they can charge you for each valuation. One line means only one fee rather than several.

CHAPTER TEN
FINANCE

Finance is a hugely important piece of the development puzzle. It's commonly known as the hardest part of modern-day property developing. Balancing equity and borrowing power is the key to success in the wake of responsible lending laws. So, while you can leave the execution to your expert team members, a thorough understanding of what's involved on the finance front will be hugely beneficial to you to expand your portfolio.

Common finance terms

The banking, insurance and superannuation industry in Australia is supervised by the Australian Prudential Regulation Authority (APRA). As part of its objective to promote stability in Australia's financial system, APRA is now limiting borrowing capacity, as well as targeting interest-only (IO) loans to protect investors from over-leveraging. This means you might have additional hurdles to jump to secure your finance. Therefore, don't trust websites with the lowest interest rates, as these rates can come with catches – restrictions on releasing equity, for example.

Non-bank lenders fall under a set of different regulations from the Australian Securities and Investments Commission (ASIC). ASIC 'regulates the conduct of Australian companies, financial markets, financial services organisations (including banks, life and general insurers and superannuation funds) and professionals who deal in and advise on investments, superannuation, insurance, deposit-taking and credit'.

In finance, there are a few acronyms to get your head around. Let's look at the main ones:

- **LMI.** You'll need to pay *lenders mortgage insurance* if you borrow more than 80 per cent of your home's value. It protects the lender, **not** the borrower.

- **LVR.** *Loan-to-value* ratio shows the value of your home loan as a percentage of the property's value. The lower the LVR, the lower the risk you pose to the bank.

- **HEM.** The banks use *household expenditure measure* to estimate your annual living expenses if you are applying for a retail loan to secure land.

- **GRV.** *Gross realisation value* is the total value of all sales at the end of a development project. This number is very important in development lending, as lenders determine how much they will lend as a percentage of the GRV (e.g. 65 per cent of GRV, pending a valuation).

- **TDC.** *Total development cost* is the sum of all costs for the proposed development. This includes what you pay for the land and the costs of development, construction, titles, finance and marketing. As with GRV, a lender will lend based on a percentage of the TDC – normally 70 or 80 per cent of TDC.

Borrowing capacity

Affordability and serviceability are two different things – the bank stress-tests loans at higher interest rates than are available at the time – so it's a good idea to understand how the bank calculates both to get your finance approved. While finance for a development can come from a range of sources (as we discuss later in this chapter) lenders will all look at your income, expenses and rental returns from the existing property on the lot (if there is one) to determine how much you can borrow. A general rule is that you can borrow around six times your income, but not all forms of income are treated equally by lenders.

As with residential property investing, any credit card debt or lines of credit will significantly hurt your capacity to borrow. Our tip is to close credit cards or reduce their limits, because even if the credit card has $0 outstanding, the bank will act as if you owe the full amount to reduce their risk. Also, avoid any personal or car loans! Banks look at how much debt you're servicing, and this will count as a black mark against you.

There are two important borrowing calculations to be aware of:

1. **Debt service ratio (DSR)** is the ratio of your loan repayments to your gross income. For most lenders, this figure should not exceed 30 per cent for singles and 40 per cent for couples.

2. **Net debt-to-income (DTI) ratio** is the ratio of your net disposable income to total debt commitments. For most lenders, this ratio must be greater than 1.25:1 – that is, your net disposable income needs to be at least 25 per cent higher than your total debt commitments.

There are generally two ways to borrow more: increase your cash flow or reduce your outgoings. You can increase your cash flow by earning more income (strive for pay rises or get a second stable job), increasing rents on existing properties in your portfolio or pursuing higher yielding properties. You can reduce your outgoings by cutting down on lifestyle costs (such as rent, entertainment and luxuries) and getting rid of credit cards and other liabilities.

Pre-approval

A pre-approval on a loan means you have your finances in order but doesn't mean you have the ability to borrow what you like. Let's make this clear: pre-approval isn't a guarantee that the bank is going to loan you that amount. Also keep in mind that if the property is in a certain postcode or of a specialised type (such as a hotel, car wash centre or petrol station), lenders may require a lower LVR, which can impact your borrowing capacity.

Here are some things you can do to help your chances:

- Limit your debt on credit cards (and resist buying furniture and accessories for the new home on credit cards), as this may be seen as a red flag by the lender.

- Maintain both your income and expenditure during the review period.

- Ensure the property you intend to buy meets the lender's criteria and is of equal or greater value than what you're paying for it.

Refinance

A refinance essentially involves entering into a new loan agreement, which you can do with your existing lender (called an 'internal refinance') or a new lender (an 'external refinance'). These restructures can provide substantial financial benefits, including locking in a better interest rate, resetting your interest-only term and resetting your loan term to 30 years.

For many developers, refinancing is the key to building a portfolio. Our advice is to refinance every two to four years. If you have equity in your first property, you can extract it to fund another property purchase. This equity could come from you paying down the debt on the property or from the property's increase in value. Your first step is to find a great mortgage broker and organise the refinance of the first property to fund the second. This loan should be pre-approved before you purchase the next property. Typically, if you have the serviceability and at least 25 per cent equity, you can draw 80 per cent of this (to keep, say, an 80 per cent loan), which will then provide a 20 per cent deposit.

Debt

It's important not to fear 'good debt', although you should be cautious about 'bad debt':

- **Bad debt** includes car loans, credit cards, home loans against owner-occupied properties (these can be good investments providing strong capital growth, but they're considered a liability for lending) and debt against liabilities that depreciate.
- **Good debt** is debt against property, investments, collectables or assets that appreciate in value.

If you're uncomfortable with the idea of holding debt, it's a good idea to flick back to the start of the book and look at your goals again. Good debt is the cornerstone of success in property developing and, like anything, involves risk. You might want to reconsider development as your wealth vehicle if you are not comfortable with the concept.

Mortgage brokers

We talked about mortgage brokers in chapter 7 – they're crucial members of your foundation team. A good mortgage broker who is well-versed in complex development finance will be much more valuable to you than a suburban broker in a retail shopping strip. You need a development-savvy broker who has experience.

A mortgage broker's job is to work through the types of loans, features and options available to you. They will go directly to multiple lenders and assess the criteria from each institution. For retail loans these criteria can relate to your ability to service the loan, the interest rate, the loan term and fees, P&I loans versus IO loans, and the use of offset accounts.

For commercial and construction loans, it's all about how financially viable the development is – this is how the lender will value it from a risk point of view. The interest rate, fee and pre-sale requirements will vary depending on how the development stacks up and your experience. An experienced broker will understand the intricacies of development finance and source an appropriate lender accordingly.

The broker will help you compare loans and choose the right loan for your development, and guide you through the loan application process. They will advocate for you if things go wrong with a lender or mortgage application, and work with major banks, non-bank lenders and private lenders – depending on which best suits your needs – and find you the most feasible lending option. In the end, it's your decision which lender to go with. Most people engage a mortgage broker because they do all the work for you and don't charge you – they're paid by the lender once a loan is obtained (though their service is usually uncompromised as most lenders will pay the broker a similar amount). Brokers will often charge a fee of 1 to 2 per cent of the loan for a development project as they're much more complex. This fee will form part of the TDC, so you don't pay it up front.

A broker will typically look at more than 20 lenders, which you may not have the skills or time to do. As they don't get paid unless they obtain a loan for you, in effect, all this upfront work is unpaid. This motivates them to find the best offer for you. Once you have the offer, you can check individual lenders' websites and comparison websites to see if it's competitive. The interest rate should not be the sole factor determining your decision; flexibility and loan features aligned with your personal circumstances, investment goals and risk profile are far more valuable to you. With hundreds of lenders all offering different products, an experienced broker can be invaluable.

Note that you should engage a broker only at the stage of making a loan application. It's best to use only one reputable broker, as you don't want them stepping on each other's toes; also, if a lender has enquiries from two brokers about the same property, it can raise red flags. However, you can speak with multiple brokers initially to find the one you'll go with.

Once you find a good broker, it's worth being loyal to them to achieve a good long-term outcome. However, not all mortgage brokers are trustworthy or competent. So, how do you find a good broker? Once you have the names of a few brokers, meet with them and ask the following questions, consider their answers and check the references they provide, and then make your choice:

- How long have you been a broker?
- What are your qualifications?
- How many residential development loans have you sourced?
- How many commercial loans for development have you secured?
- How many lenders do you have access to?
- What makes you choose one lender over another?
- Do you have three recent clients you can provide as references?
- Can you provide details of some recent, similar finance deals you have secured for other developers?
- What are your broker fees?

How does GST work?

If you are in the business of selling property, as most property developers are, you can use the 'margin scheme' to calculate the GST you need to pay on the sale, which can reduce the amount of GST you need to pay. To be eligible to use the margin scheme you must be registered for GST; the sale of the property must be a taxable supply; and when you originally purchased the property, you did not pay GST. (A taxable supply will include a charge for GST. A supplier makes a taxable supply if they are registered for GST and the supply is: for consideration; and made in the course of an enterprise carrying on their business; and connected with Australia.)

There are tools at ato.gov.au that you can use to help confirm whether or not you are eligible for the margin scheme, as well as examples that can assist you in calculating the margin. The two calculation methods are the consideration method and the valuation method.

Consideration method

The consideration method can be used to determine the GST payable under the margin scheme regardless of when you purchased the property you are now selling. This method calculates the difference between the end sale price and the initial purchase price. You also can't include any settlement adjustments in the sales contract, or any legal fees, stamp duty, costs for developing the property, option agreements or any other purchase-related expenses.

Valuation method

The valuation method can be used when you hold an approved valuation if you originally purchased the property before 1 July 2000. Using this method, the margin will be the difference between the sale price and the value of the property at 1 July 2000.

Normally, the amount of GST paid on a property sale will be one-eleventh of the total sale price. It's also important to note that you can't claim back a GST credit when buying a property if the margin scheme was used. If you originally purchased a property and were charged the full rate of GST, the margin scheme can't be used when you sell it; this is because you would have claimed back the GST as part of your business.

As of 1 July 2018, when purchasing a taxable supply of a new residential property or land, in most cases the purchaser will pay at settlement both the withheld amount of GST directly to the ATO and the balance of the sale price (minus the withholding amount to the supplier).

The purchaser must also withhold and remit to the ATO the following amounts:

- one-eleventh of the sale price (for taxable supplies)
- 7 per cent of the contract price (for margin scheme supplies)
- 10 per cent of GST-exclusive market value of the supply (for supplies between associates for a price less than GST-inclusive market value).

In addition, a business activity statement (BAS) must still be lodged by the supplier, and they must report their GST liabilities or entitlements or taxable supplies of these types of properties.

Steve and Liam's tips

As you can see, this can get very complex, and this is not financial advice! Your accountant or property lawyer who specialises in this will be able to provide the right advice for you regarding GST. You can also speak with the ATO to obtain rulings to assist you in understanding GST implications.

Accounting horror story

A client with 20 years' experience as a builder decided to try his hand at development – starting with a development of townhouses in southwest Sydney. But development inexperience can create problems, and by not seeking any legal, tax or professional advice, doing a feasibility analysis or speaking to an accountant about how building townhouses works, he found himself in some trouble. When time and cost delays began to blow out, he was forced to seek out family and friends to loan him money to finish the project, as well as the buyer, who threw him a lifeline. Sadly, he also had to sell his home. But he went on to finish it, and all was fine until a few years after, when the ATO decided to audit him. He hadn't kept any records or documents – bank statements, receipts and invoices, feasibility analysis, contract of sales or proof of income. This meant he had to pay more tax than he should have because he didn't have proof that the loans were in fact loans, cash deposits or income. As he hadn't accounted for GST, the ATO taxed the money received, and he lost of a lot of money. The smarter solution would have been to lock in the best buying structure – and, of course, seek the right advice. You need to ensure you have great money management, invoicing and receipt systems.

Finance for developments

Generally, there are three types of finance for developments: retail, commercial and construction. They differ greatly when it comes to costs, requirements and assessment to secure. It's important to understand the difference so you can set yourself up correctly from the start.

The process for financing a development generally comprises two stages:

1. land acquisition, which is generally a retail loan via a bank or non-bank (but can be a commercial loan)
2. construction, which is a construction loan via a bank, non-bank or private lending. You'll only ever have one loan at a time, so the retail or commercial loan will cease and the construction loan commence when you go into the construction phase.

There are some exceptions, such as when you purchase a site with an existing DA. In this scenario, you only ever hold a construction loan.

Development finance can involve multiple layers of debt and equity that form the 'capital stack'. The capital stack is the structure of all the funding raised for a development project, including common equity provided by developers and the various forms of debt sourced from different lenders.

How that debt or equity sits will determine how much risk there is. The chart shows how lenders will lend against either TDC or GRV and what returns each party can expect in the current market.

The capital stack

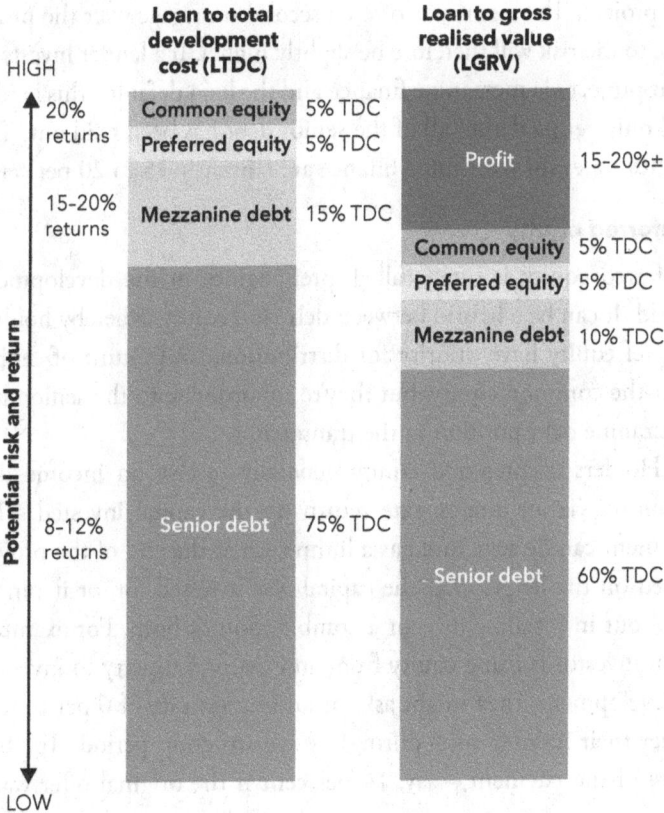

	Loan to total development cost (LTDC)		Loan to gross realised value (LGRV)	
HIGH				
20% returns	Common equity	5% TDC	Profit	15–20%±
	Preferred equity	5% TDC		
15–20% returns	Mezzanine debt	15% TDC		
			Common equity	5% TDC
			Preferred equity	5% TDC
			Mezzanine debt	10% TDC
8–12% returns	Senior debt	75% TDC	Senior debt	60% TDC
LOW				

Potential risk and return (vertical axis label)

Now, let's take a look at the layers within the capital stack.

Senior debt

Senior debt sits at the base of the capital stack and makes up anywhere between 60 and 75 per cent of the project in terms of funding. As a result, senior debt has the highest level of security in the form of a first registered mortgage over the property, which means the interest rate will be the lowest – anywhere from 8 to 12 per cent.

Mezzanine debt

Mezzanine debt sits above senior debt. This loan can help stretch the capital stack to a higher percentage of TDC or GRV to help fund the project. The security is often a second mortgage over the property, so the risk will therefore be slightly higher. If a lender invests in your project via mezzanine finance and the loan defaults, this lender will only get paid after all of the senior debt has been paid out. The interest rates for mezzanine finance are currently 15 to 20 per cent.

Preferred equity

Preferred equity is often called 'pref' equity in the development world. It can be a hybrid between debt and equity, whereby holders of pref equity have priority for distributions and return of capital over the common equity, but they're subordinate to the senior and mezzanine debt position in the transaction.

Holders of preferred equity generally receive an income distribution via an interest-rate return on the capital invested. This payment can be structured as a lump sum at the end of the project based on the length that the capital was invested for, or it can be paid out in instalments – or a combination of both. For example, if an investor is using equity from an existing property to invest in a development, they might ask for an interest rate of 6 per cent to cover their interest costs during the construction period. The balance of the payment – say, 14 per cent if the original offer was a 20 per cent interest-rate return on the capital invested – would be paid on completion.

Common equity

Common equity sits at the top of the capital stack and has the highest risk but also the highest potential for returns. It can either be your equity or a combination of yours and investors', and it can be sourced from family, friends, colleagues, high-net-worth individuals or private equity institutions. Having access to this equity will allow you to keep moving forward with more projects, and if done successfully will allow you to expand your business through having repeat investors.

Common equity is the first pool of money to go into the deal and is often referred to as having 'skin in the game'. The return for common equity is the profit at the end of the project. In terms of a cash-on-cash return, this can be upwards of 100 per cent!

Another way of structuring this is where you partner with an investor who contributes the common equity; the profit would then generally be split 50/50 between the developer and the equity partner. The equity partner and the developer have a registered interest over the land – they are both mortgage holders and are both on the title. It's important that you're clear on where the responsibilities lie in this relationship; this should be documented clearly through a legal agreement. As the developer, you want full control of the decision-making throughout the process when it comes to sourcing the deal, getting finance, managing the project, appointing builders and negotiating with buyers. Both the developer and equity partner will be loan guarantors.

***

Upon completion of the development, there will be a defined process for payments, which is commonly referred to as a 'waterfall' payment: the senior debt is paid out first, followed by the mezzanine debt, preferred equity, common equity and profit.

CHAPTER ELEVEN
BUYING STRUCTURES

There are many ways to structure a development project. Deciding on the best ownership structure can be a confusing and complex process, but it's vital to get this right, because it can save you thousands of dollars in tax and protect your personal assets in the event of bankruptcy. A good development-savvy accountant will be your best friend here.

In this book, we focus on the four most common structures, as these will most likely be the structures you'll use (the more advanced structures, such as using mezzanine debt, syndicates and hybrid models, are best left to advanced developers):

1. Doing a development by yourself, either as an individual or a company.

2. Doing a development with a money or loan partner as a joint venture (JV).

3. Doing a development with an equity partner as a JV.

4. Doing a development with a landowner as a project development agreement (PDA) or development management agreement (DMA).

Let's look at these in more detail.

Doing a development by yourself

You can do a development by yourself either as an individual or a company.

Individual

Doing a property development in your own name is the simplest and most common method – it has no set-up cost and minimal compliance. It also has the benefit of allowing you to negatively gear the development if there are any losses.

However, if the development is positively geared, this may not be particularly beneficial: the positive cash flow is added onto your salary and other personal income, which might cause you to have to pay much more tax. The profit on completion of the development would also be retained by you as an individual, likely resulting in a higher percentage of the profit being taken by tax. Also, you could lose the property if you become bankrupt, even if your debts don't relate to the property. If anything were to go wrong during the project, with the builder or anyone else involved, you as an individual would also be liable, leaving you open to being sued for damages.

Company

A company is a legal entity in its own right; when you borrow in the name of a company, it will own the investment property. The company will be the borrower, and all the directors of the company will be required to guarantee the loan.

Some of the benefits of buying under a company structure include a lower tax rate, the ability to plan tax through dividends, the fact that the tax paid by the company can be franked – that is, passed on as credit to shareholders with dividends – and the fact that it provides a much higher level of protection for your assets outside the company.

However, financing is usually harder for companies to obtain due to banking restrictions, and you risk losing the property if your company is sued. Some other drawbacks are that the set-up and maintenance costs of a company structure are quite high, and companies aren't eligible for the 50 per cent discount on capital gains available to trusts and individuals. A company can't distribute losses, either, so this isn't a suitable structure if your property is negatively geared. Another issue is that although you won't be personally liable for the company's debts as a director, you'll be legally obligated for responsibilities such as ensuring solvent trading.

Doing a development with a JV partner

There are two types of JV partner – loan partners, who inject capital as a loan and receive an interest rate on the money invested into the project, or equity partners, who inject capital as equity and become part of the ownership structure with profit share. You could do a development with either of these, or possibly both!

To make either arrangement work, you'll need to agree on a structure and outline the responsibilities. You'll need advice from a business or property accountant to get the right tax structure in place. Then, a property lawyer is required to draw up the loan agreement. As the developer, you'll want to control the decision-making process, but to keep your partner happy it's vital to update them as the project progresses.

Ideally, you would have partners lined up before securing deals. You don't have a long time to find partners once the deal is under contract, but securing a property under an option will allow you more time. You'll need to know the capital required, the interest on the capital and when the partner will be paid the interest (monthly or at settlement), as well as the required security and financial guarantees.

Also, it's a good idea to know how to market yourself to create a strong impression in the industry as a reputable developer. Develop your branding with a business name, business cards, a website and a social media presence, and have an information booklet ready to distribute in the form of an e-book. Spend time networking and attending events, because being known will make it easier to secure trust and funding when the time comes.

Doing a development with a money or loan partner

A good way to think about the relationship with a money or loan partner is that you as the developer contribute your time and knowledge, while the partner contributes the necessary funds. They simply lend you money – they're not on the title or loan.

The project will pay the money partner an interest-rate return on their money, and they will generally secure their position by way of a second-tier mortgage and possibly a personal guarantee. If you're unable to offer a second-tier mortgage, the level of risk will be higher for the money partner, so you could look at offering a higher interest rate. The higher the risk, the higher the return should be. Try to think about it from the investor's point of view and structure a deal that works for all parties.

You'll need to understand when the funds will be required – if you have the funds too early, you'll end up paying more interest over the length of time the money is invested.

Self-managed superannuation funds (SMSF) can be great sources of capital for development projects. Likewise, development projects can also be hugely beneficial for investors as they can increase their super fund balance at a faster rate than standard industry funds. One point to note, though, is that an investment with an SMSF property must be third-party and not related to you.

Doing a development with an equity partner

An equity partner injects capital as equity and becomes part of the ownership structure with a profit share. In this model, you as the developer contribute time and knowledge, and the equity partner contributes necessary equity (and you could contribute some equity as well).

In most cases, a unit trust is the best structure with an equity partner. If you're securing the property under a normal retail loan, you'll generally both need to be on the title, but there can be exceptions. If the equity partner is funding the project without input financially from you as the developer, you may not need to be on the title or even the unit trust; you could manage this under a DMA or PDA instead.

You'll need to agree on project management fees for the developer (are these paid monthly or quarterly?) and profit share. Note that profit share is often the last item to be agreed.

Doing a development with a landowner

This is one of our favourite types of structure! There are so many advantages to developing with a landowner, but you need to be very careful how the agreement is drawn up. Be sure to engage an experienced property lawyer who understands these types of transactions to ensure the necessary inclusions and securities are within the PDA.

Technically, this isn't a joint venture, as the landowner is effectively employing you as the developer to develop their property for them. You don't want it to be deemed by the ATO as a 'partnership', as this can bring unwanted tax to the equation: the seller could be up for capital gains tax (CGT), and there could be stamp duty charges if it's deemed a partnership, which you want to avoid.

The big benefit to you as the developer in this scenario is that you can complete the development without ever actually owning the property. This offers huge savings in terms of stamp duty and interest costs.

The big benefit to the landowner is that they can achieve a higher price for the sale of their property by offering it up to be developed and then taking a share in the profit. The landowner may also want to keep part of the development. This can be good for downsizers, who like the location but would like a lower-maintenance property; developing a duplex on their site, allowing them to hold one and sell the other, is a fantastic outcome for all parties.

One of the key factors in making this work is having low or no debt on the site. The land would be offered up as security for the development and the equity within it absorbed by the lender to contribute towards funding the project.

Once the development is completed, the landowner gets the land value pre-agreed at commencement plus a share in the profits. You as the developer get a share in the profits without ever owning the property!

CHAPTER TWELVE
BRINGING THE DEAL TOGETHER

Before you buy your site and start filling out your feasibility numbers, how you do ensure you're getting the best and most appropriate information to pull it all together?

Leaning on your wider team

You'll need to speak with local agents to understand the value of the site acquisition price. Note that the zoning can change, which can affect the price dramatically. Ensure you aren't paying too much just because the seller believes the zoning may change in the future.

The titles office in your state or territory will help you understand if there are any caveats, encumbrances or easements, while your town planner will help you understand your best use for the land and assist you in obtaining development approval for your proposed project.

Your mortgage broker will confirm how much you can borrow to finance the project (based on your feasibility), and your architect will give you a quote for a concept site plan that will fit the topography and restrictions of the site.

Finally, your builder will give you an estimate of what the construction works will cost and how long you can expect it to take to reach completion. (Remember to factor in interest rates and other holding costs.) Using square-metre rates is a common way to get estimates from builders, so you'll need to know the size of the building you're planning on completing. Note that the builder's price will be based on measurements from external wall to external wall, and a lot of the floor plans you see from architects measure from internal wall to internal wall. Furthermore, areas such as garages, balconies and voids aren't included in gross floor areas and can be missed in the initial estimates. Be sure to give your builder as much information as possible to get an accurate estimate for the build cost.

After completion, your selling agent will have a high-level understanding of achievable prices for that area (based on comparable sales) and can help you market the properties for sale.

Using software to help build your feasibility

There are some fantastic software programs and websites available to help you with your due diligence and feasibility. Council websites can vary significantly – some are great, while others are terrible! Subscription-based websites such as Landchecker, RP Data and Nearmap are fantastic for getting up-to-date information on zoning, nearby developments, easements, lot sizes and so on. More detailed, premium software such as ARGUS EstateMaster or ARGUS Developer, Devfeas and Archistar are more expensive and probably not essential unless you're constantly looking at multiple sites and completing multiple projects a year.

Microsoft Excel is a common program to run feasibility studies. The benefit is that you can set up multiple tabs and build your initial feasibility, cash flow requirements, program, sensitivity analysis and overall summary in one place. Banks love to see these types of documents as part of their review of the project when it comes to lending.

As you move from the hypothetical and educated assumptions to the most reliable quotes with detailed feasibility, you must become more accurate to ensure your data input, predictions and economic viability are worth the risk. As you proceed with the development, you should be eliminating assumptions and substantiating the estimates. (This also relates to the sensitivity analysis, creative financing and consideration of sales prices and rental rates.)

Constantly exploring ways to decrease costs and increase revenue over time will only increase your project's net income. Remember, it's important to reduce costs where possible without reducing quality for the buyer – the quality of your work will set your reputation and can make or break future success. Don't cut corners!

Getting ready to purchase

As you complete your detailed feasibility and get ready to buy a site, there are a few items you'll need to check before you go unconditional on a contract. Then, you'll need to understand how pricing works so you can secure the best deal and set yourself up for success during the negotiations.

Before going unconditional on a contract, your solicitor or conveyancer can assist you in determining a few things:

- The seller has the authority to sell
- The property does not violate any government regulations
- Utilities are available to the property
- Soil and environmental conditions are acceptable (check that the site was never used as landfill or a repository for toxic waste)
- You're aware of any liabilities that encumber the property, such as overlays or easements

- There are no court proceedings relating to the property
- There are no plans for road widening that will reduce your land size
- There are no outstanding leases preventing you from developing
- You have the required equity, financing and project viability to complete the project.

There are many factors affecting the purchase price of a block. This section covers the main factors.

Block size

The size and shape of the block can drastically change the site's value as well as how much you can develop on it. Obviously, a bigger block will be worth more due to its land value, but not all blocks are made equally. An irregular-sized site can have complicated planning repercussions, which may mean fewer dwellings and more wasted 'garden' and fencing areas than a rectangular block.

Slope

The more the block slopes, the more expensive it will be to build on. This is because the work required with excavation, retaining walls and drainage issues all adds complexity. Generally, properties with a gentle slope towards the street will have a cheaper build price, as pipework will flow towards the mains on the street due to gravity. This is particularly important for sewerage.

Frontage

A wider frontage can help you comply with council guidelines; for example, some require a minimum 15-metre frontage for a dual occupancy. If you require access down the side of either an existing house or a new dwelling, the wider frontage will ensure you have enough width to accommodate the construction of, and access to, new dwellings at the rear.

Existing dwellings

Do you retain the existing dwelling, renovate it or demolish it? A cheap renovation can improve value without having to demolish and then build from scratch. Where the existing dwelling is located on the block is critical – if you can design around it, this can be highly advantageous, even from a GST perspective on the sale (but get your accountant to confirm). Understanding what the existing building has been constructed from is also important – if it contains asbestos and you plan to demolish it, you'll need to allow for this in your demolition budget.

Soil type

The soil type will determine what design is required for the foundation or slab. A geotechnical engineer will generally be the expert to confirm this. There are different classes; here are the common types:

- **A - Acceptable (0mm movement).** These are often sites where the slab is founded on rock or sand.
- **S - Satisfactory (0-20mm movement).** Generally, these are sites on a clay foundation that is only slightly reactive and minimal movement is expected.
- **M - Moderately reactive (20-40mm movement).** These sites are similar to 'satisfactory', with the exception being the clay (or silty clay) is more reactive to moisture, which will result in moderate ground movement.
- **H - Highly reactive (40-60mm movement).** These are clay sites where the material is highly reactive, resulting in more movement.
- **E - Extremely reactive (60-75mm movement).** These are clay sites with the potential for the highest amount of movement.
- **P - Problem (movement unknown).** These are sites that are sloping, have loose or collapsing soils, or are subject to erosion or high moisture. Consequently, a specific foundation will need

to be designed, perhaps involving deep piers or retaining walls with provisions for drainage.

Trees

The location, species, height and diameter of trees can impact a development site. An arborist is a specialist who determines the health of trees on a site and can make recommendations as to whether trees can be removed. It's also important to consider root zones from neighbouring properties as these can affect the foundations on your potential site. If a tree that can't be removed is located where you require a driveway to be constructed, for example, this may mean the site is no longer feasible. The same goes for trees that are protected and would need to be removed to make room for a new dwelling.

Titling and council regulations and zonings

The zoning of the site is very important, and you need to understand fully what is possible on the site in line with council regulations. A site that allows for higher-density building can be more expensive as a result.

Easements, overlays and covenants

Any easement, overlay or covenant over the site have the potential to restrict what it is possible to design and build over the site. Some easements can be designed around, while others are highly restrictive and can prevent any profitable development. Heritage overlays may result in a development no longer being feasible as the existing dwelling can't be removed.

Noise

Where properties are located near trains or airports, for example, you'll need to consider noise mitigation in future designs. This can result in hidden build costs that don't necessarily improve value.

Precedence

Council websites are a great source of information when it comes to seeing what other developments have been approved nearby. Going for a drive around the area will also give you an idea of what council is approving in terms of development. Sometimes a council may have a standard rule for setback from side boundaries, which could restrict development opportunities. As you drive around the streets, you might see that setbacks are closer than council guidelines. This can be because council wants to maintain the streetscape and set a precedent in the area, and not have a bunch of random developments with varying designs.

Infrastructure contributions

New development requires contributions to be paid to council. Knowing the cost of these based on the council and proposed development is important.

Negotiating the purchase

When you're ready to purchase, you need to understand how to play the game. Remember, as a developer, overpaying kills your profits, and a bargain sets you up for a huge win. Here are our tips for handling this crucial stage of your development.

Make personal contact

Calling the agent will always yield better results than cold emailing. A great opener is, 'I'm doing my research on a similar property in [nearby area], but I like the look of your listing too, and I can see this property valued at [amount justified by the recent sale of a similar property]. Would I be wasting my time with an offer like that?' Following this, they may tell you the lowest price the seller will accept or confirm it's worth negotiating further. Alternatively, if the agent isn't interested, that shows they've had buyer interest exceeding this price.

Don't lowball – reasonable offers will always gain more respect from agents. This is also an opportunity to develop a relationship with the agent, even if you don't secure this particular property.

Understand what's negotiable

You can negotiate not only on price but also on conditions. These include settlement period, agreements, early access, building and pest inspections, finance periods, deposit amounts, subject to development approval (DA) and whether or not a portion of your deposit is refundable. Don't use too many conditions if you don't have to, or if you know you can pay cash and can go unconditional on the sale, because then you put yourself above those offering the same price but who are dependent on finance. You can also put an 'option' on a property, as we explained in chapter 8.

Understand what's happening behind the scenes

If you know the seller might want to sell to buy another property but still wants to be in the area until the other property is built, you could negotiate a lower price, even if others are offering more, providing that you rent it back to them for six months. Check how long the property has been on the market and if it's failed at auction previously, as this will indicate whether there's an opportunity to make a lower offer. Likewise, if a property you enquired about when it was first listed has sat on the market longer than expected, it may represent an opportunity that wasn't there when it was first listed.

Ask questions to understand the seller's motives and situation

Asking the right questions the right way can help you read between the lines and find out what's going on. Pay close attention to what you're told when you ask these questions:

- Why is the vendor selling?
- Who owns it? (A private individual or a company?)

- Is the vendor after a short or long settlement period?
- How long has it been on the market?
- What's the lowest price the vendor will accept? (Take the answer to this with a grain of salt.)
- Apart from the listing price, what would the perfect offer look like to the vendor?
- Is the property occupied? Where will the owners move to?
- Is the owner willing to participate in the development in return for part of the completed development or part of the profit? (This would be a joint venture with landowner arrangement – see chapter 11.)

Manage your behaviour

Ignore people who say it's better to be aggressive. Nope! Being confident and polite shows you understand the process and aren't emotionally invested. This comes by understanding what the seller wants and removing their problems. It will also mean the agent is willing to work with you again whether or not you secure the initial deal. Creating win-win scenarios is often the key to negotiating well. Use your knowledge to help problem-solve, and always act professionally.

Keep your options open

Remember to look at multiple properties at the same time so that you don't become attached to one property and have to outbid for it. Determine the price that you'll walk away at. Mentioning other properties to the seller will also encourage them to play ball as they might feel the fear of missing out.

Listen well

Be a good listener and communicator. Hear what the other party wants (particularly when you are dealing with the owner directly), clearly outline your points and look for a win-win in all scenarios.

Try to deal with the decision-maker (that is, the landowner) directly, if possible, as this will ensure that the negotiation is quick and nothing is miscommunicated.

Understand the seller's priorities

The seller might want a lot of things, but you need to find out what their non-negotiables are and understand what you can afford to give away or be flexible on.

Wrap everything up

Summarise what has been agreed via emails to ensure it's clear. Also, at the end of each meeting, try and summarise verbally what has been discussed to confirm the main points or agreements.

Back yourself

If you're turned away by the agent at the price you believe it's worth, save the listing and keep an eye on it. Always understand the property's value, and be prepared to walk away. If you see the property still on the market down the track, you can contact the agent again, as they might be more willing to negotiate now.

Leave the door open

If you have to walk away, tell the agent the price you need to see to become an active bidder again. This lets them know you're open to future negotiation or deals.

Setting yourself up for settlement

Ensure the contract is subject to finance and subject to due diligence if required. Having an unconditional contract is sometimes favourable for getting the best price, but you'll need to do all your work up front! If you're not confident with this, work out how long you may need for the due diligence period depending on the complexity of the deal so that you have enough time to evaluate and fully inspect the property. It's not always possible but, if you can make the contract subject to DA, this is a huge benefit. This is more likely to get approved for larger projects or greenfield projects where the yield takes time to calculate and DA is critical for the deal to go ahead.

Speak to an accountant about the name you'll purchase under – your own or that of an entity. Always have an experienced conveyancer or solicitor review the contract, too.

Speak to a broker to make sure you have finances approved, and prepare costs, such as the deposit, stamp duty, mortgage fees, registration costs, survey costs and solicitor fees. In most cases, you'll be buying a raw development site – a site that doesn't have an approval. This means you're buying an investment property, so keep this in mind when it comes to finance, because you could be seeking a normal retail loan or potentially a commercial loan. You'll also need money for DA. Once DA is approved, you'll likely move to a construction loan to obtain finance until the project is completed. Lenders consider properties with more than three titles a commercial property, and the loans will reflect this; a duplex, for example, can be under a standard residential loan.

PART V
EXECUTING THE
DEVELOPMENT

I f you've made it this far, congratulations – this is when your development starts to come to life and there's no turning back!

This is the part of the journey when people can jump to images of developers cruising up to their project in a flash car, surveying the landscape heroically with a latte in hand. While it's exciting to get to the point when you're ready to start building, sadly it's not the reality for most to just sit back and let it all happen. It's when the fun really starts! Key to building a successful development that starts and finishes on time and on budget is understanding where everything fits in, lining up the right people for the job and allowing for things to go wrong or be delayed. You're in this for the best part of up to three years, which means plenty of time for things to happen or change. Some things will always be out of your control, but if you can create some breathing room in your schedule and a cash buffer, you'll set yourself up to succeed every time.

CHAPTER THIRTEEN
STARTING YOUR DEVELOPMENT

To start construction, you'll need to hold development and/or building approval. Securing these permits can take up to nine months.

Let's delve into development approval (DA) and building approval (BA) so you can see what's involved.

Development approval

Essentially, a development permit is a legal document that allows you to undertake a development. It relates to the proposed use of the land and is awarded by the relevant council. (The exception to this is if you're in NSW, where you can obtain a Complying Development Certificate, or CDC. This is an assessment by a council or accredited certifier that is fast-tracked when the proposed development meets certain guidelines stipulated by the NSW Department of Planning & Environment. It is designed to boost housing supply in the state.)

The key people in your team for your DA are your architect, town planner, landscape architect and civil engineer. You'll need multiple meetings with all of them. It can be useful for your architect to instruct the surveyor on what they need to pick up in their detailed survey, and they will often work together with your town planner. It's best to choose professionals who have worked together before and work well together. They're likely to recommend one another, too.

Special reports may also be required depending on the project, as discussed in chapter 6. Once these reports are complete, you can provide your architect with a design brief, but remember: architects can't provide DA, just the design, so don't ask them for a DA. Essentially, you want to provide them with all the information they need to design something you and the market want. This is where your market research will be critical, and you should go into the DA process having completed due diligence and with a clear understanding of what you want to build.

Here's the DA process in a nutshell:

1. Obtain a yield analysis or massing plan (how much you can build on the site).
2. Perform feasibility.
3. Determine the most profitable use of the land.
4. Prepare initial DA plans.
5. Consult agents on marketability.
6. Consult builders on constructability.
7. Consider conducting a pre-lodgement meeting with council.
8. Finalise the plans and the town planning report.
9. Lodge your application with council.
10. Respond to requests for information (RFIs).
11. Review and accept or challenge conditions.
12. Appeal (if necessary).

Steve and Liam's tips

More apartments or townhouses doesn't always mean more profit. Basements are very expensive to build, especially for apartment buildings, so it may not be the **highest and best use** of a site to design an underground car park with more apartment levels. At-ground parking with fewer levels may offer a higher profit margin. We can tell you firsthand from our engineering days that suspended slabs and cantilevers are also expensive to construct, as are multiple step-downs or level changes. Construction joints in slabs and multiple pours increase time and costs, which transfers onto the frame, roofing, plastering and painting. Voids in the design may be impressive, but you forgo additional floor space upstairs, which means missing out on the increased marketability and selling price of an extra bedroom or study nook. Avoid these when possible.

Double-check all the conditions of the DA and pay all required council contributions. The DA will detail the site management plans, environmental management plans, traffic and pedestrian access, working hours, and waste management and noise and vibration requirements. In addition, there are processes to follow for any unexpected finds once works commence, such as contaminated soil or First Nations artefacts. This is an extremely important document, so ensure your nominated builder is also aware of the requirements under the approval.

Building approval

Once you have your DA, you'll next need your BA (or CC, if you're in NSW). The BA relates to all construction on your site, covering operational works, plumbing and drainage approval. If demolition is required, you might need a demolition permit too, or you might need a relocation permit if the existing dwelling is being shifted on the site.

Your BA/CC team will comprise an architect, structural engineer, civil engineer, hydraulic engineer, geotechnical engineer, mechanical engineer, electrical engineer, fire engineer and building certifier. We covered this in more detail in chapter 6, but here's a quick rundown of your people's most important roles:

- Architects need to work through the drawings and provide further detail, dimensions and cross-sections. Once complete, these working drawings can then be passed on to engineers for review. Engineers can't start their work until the architect has provided the drawings.

- Civil engineers confirm earthworks, levels for slabs, services, stormwater and sewers, while hydraulic engineers design anything to do with water, working with civil engineers.

- Soil testing is passed on to the structural engineer for the slab design and decisions around whether any piers are required.

- Mechanical engineers manage ventilation to design extraction units, particularly with basements or internal bathrooms where they need to design a path for ventilation. They will also design lifts, if required.

- Electrical engineers design lighting.

- Fire engineers are required for apartment blocks. They design firefighting equipment, pumps and fire walls.

- Building certifiers confirm that all these tasks have been completed and meet industry standards and council requirements.

Steve and Liam's tips

The design brief is important for the architect and will affect the development if you make simple mistakes. Ensure that details such as air conditioning (ducted or reverse cycle), cooking (gas or electric), hot water (centralised, electric or gas), storage (under stairs or kitchen around extractor units) are resolved. Furthermore, while your plans may be sufficient for building approval, the detail may not be enough for the builder; ensure you provide the necessary detail as the design progresses to avoid rework and paying consultants more money. Lastly, lock everyone into timeframes and hold them accountable. The prices may be cheaper, but how long have they allowed? Sometimes, it could be better to pay a higher price and get a quicker turnaround. Remember, time is money!

CHAPTER FOURTEEN
COMMENCING THE BUILD

Once you have your DA and/or BA, you can commence your development.

Site meeting

The first step when commencing construction is to have a site meeting. Key consultants such as architects, surveyors and your builder must be at this meeting to go look at the site and all of the details, and confirm a construction commencement date.

The identification survey is a critical component when commencing construction. It sets out the boundaries of the proposed development, along with any other key items such as existing utilities.

Whether during this initial site meeting or just before, it's always a good idea to go and meet the neighbours adjoining your development. If the development was up for comment and feedback on the council website, you may already be aware how well your project will be received in the neighbourhood. By meeting the neighbours early on, you can introduce yourself and the builder and advise them of what will be happening, at what times and over what duration.

Timelines

By this point you'll have a building contract signed by a builder and agreed timelines. As the developer, you should also have a detailed program developed from start to finish. Within this program there will be key inspections required from external consultants, such as from council, engineers, certifiers and utility providers. Communication will be key between you and the builder as to when these inspections will take place and who organises them; it's best to make this clear from the start.

Arguably the most important timeline, and the hardest to keep track of, is the utility providers and their connections. The lead times for getting these contractors on site are lengthy, and the paperwork needs to be spot on for them to lift a finger. You could have construction completed except for gas, electricity, telecommunications or water being connected. The more notice you can give these providers, and the more informed you can keep them, the higher the chance you have of getting them out to site to complete connections so you can eventually obtain titles and sell your project.

Work as executed drawings

One of the most critical components of a development is the Work As Executed (WAE) drawings that the builder will need to compile during the project. As part of this, a surveyor will need to pick up or survey stormwater inverts, drainage pit heights, utility connections and slab heights. For the plans to be certified on completion and titles issued, this information has to be provided and checked. If there are inaccuracies or incomplete works, this can result in delays and additional costs and hinder your ability to eventually sell the development.

Progress claims

Throughout construction there will be stages when the builder will request payment. Your financier will also have their own process for releasing payment, so ensure you and your broker are clear on what this entails and what information the financier will require. For a typical residential development, the builder will expect payment upon completion of the following stages:

- Slab completion
- Frames up
- Internal fixing
- Enclosure
- Completion.

All these stages have a 'retention' held back from each payment. Generally, it will be 5 per cent, and upon completion, when all works are certified, the retention money will be released. This holds the builder accountable to ensure they complete the work to a high standard, and if there are any outstanding works at the end that the builder is refusing to come back and complete, the retention money can be withheld to complete those works. This can also apply to any defects.

Generally, if the builder has achieved practical completion, you'll release half of the retention money held and retain the remainder for what is called the defects liability period (DLP). The timeframe for this will be specified in the contract and is usually six to 12 months. During this time, if any defects arise then the builder is responsible for coming back and fixing those defects. If they don't come back, then you have the legal right to use those retained funds to fix the defects.

You can engage a quantity surveyor (QS) to quantify the works completed at various stages. They will then provide a report, which can be passed onto the financier for sign-off and release of payment to the builder. If some of the works aren't completed for a particular stage, payment can be withheld or delayed until the works are completed. For this reason, engaging a QS who is not affiliated with the builder is helpful, because when it comes to money you want to avoid arguments and a disgruntled builder.

Progress meetings

During construction, it's important to define how frequently meetings will be conducted on-site with the builder. If you have investors involved in a project, it's very important to keep them well informed of progress too, and these meetings allow you to gather the information necessary for this.

You'll want to discuss with the builder how they're progressing and ask about any issues they can foresee, such as delays with trades or wet weather. Progress meetings also provide an opportunity for you to inspect their work and ensure it's to the standard agreed. Keep a close eye on how clean and tidy the site is, as this can be a good indicator of the builder's attention to detail and organisational skills.

At these progress meetings, try and problem-solve with the builder while also holding them accountable for things that are within their control. If there are genuine reasons for an extension of time (EOT), the builder should apply for this as per the building contract, and you as the developer can then either accept or reject their request based on the circumstances.

Another item for discussion could be additional works that the builder believes they're having to do over and above what the contract or drawings stipulate. A common occurrence is uncovering rock when excavating the foundation. In some contracts, there may be a pre-agreed rate the builder receives for excavating rock, but if not then you'll need to agree on the additional cost with the builder on site.

As construction nears completion, it's very important that you check what's been installed versus what's on the plans. The builder may miss a detail, such as a certain flooring type or size of tile required. We've even had a situation where a builder put a door in the wrong spot because they thought it looked better in another location!

Take plenty of photos and notes at these onsite meetings to document them. You can use the photos when updating investors, as they love to see physical progress and feel confident that their investment is going well.

The more frequent these meetings are, the more on top of the program both you and the builder will be.

Project management

When it comes to physically doing the development, there are varying levels of involvement you can take. Whether you take on the project management yourself or outsource it depends on your experience, time availability or the financials of the project.

A project manager is someone appointed to manage the project for you. This involves communicating with architects, builders, engineers, surveyors and certifiers once the development has obtained approval. They will be heavily focused on managing every detail of the construction of the project, including documentation, coordination, tender, procurement, contract, program and cost. Their key role is to deliver the project on budget and on time. Generally, their background is in construction, engineering or architecture.

The project manager will have intricate knowledge of the approvals that have been obtained for the project and ensure that all the requirements are met. This can include providing management plans, and ensuring works are completed during the hours specified in the approval, noise limitations are adhered to and inspections are taking place during construction, whether with council directly or with consultants such as engineers, surveyors or certifiers.

A good project manager will also take care of procurement for you, such as for consultants, builders, materials and service providers. Often, service providers are extremely slow when it comes to responding to requests for information or arranging their own subcontractors to complete utility connections such as water, electricity and communications, which has the potential to substantially delay completion if your project manager is not across this.

CHAPTER FIFTEEN
PRACTICAL COMPLETION

Practical completion (PC) is the critical stage in property development when all the work has been done according to the various contracts and drawings in place, and it's ready to be occupied and used for its intended purpose. Obtaining PC requires attention to detail and a great paper trail. You'll also have to make decisions based on what you want to do with your development, and this kickstarts another facet of development – the marketing.

Key sign-offs

Once all the work has been completed, you'll need to gather sign-offs from several parties.

Permit conditions

Referring to the development permit, there are dozens of conditions the relevant council will have specified that need to be met to satisfy council and ultimately obtain sign-off. These are:

- service connections and compliance statements
- completed works driveways, kerb and gutter, and crossovers
- civil works such as stormwater, retaining walls and earthworks
- landscaping.

Insurance

Once the new buildings have been completed, insurance cover needs to be taken out for building insurance. The builder's insurance will change hands at this point.

Strata / body corporate

If you're strata-titling the development, a body corporate will need to be established to ultimately manage the complex, take over insurances and manage fees and charges. The body corporate will need to be in place at settlement.

Legals

As settlement approaches, you'll need to notify your solicitor or conveyancer. If you have off-the-plan contracts, those buyers will be advised that PC has been achieved. The predetermined settlement timeframe in those contracts will then commence, which allows buyers to ready themselves with any financiers for settlement.

Any legal agreements, such as a section 173, will also need to be completed. This is an agreement made between the council and the landowner under the *Planning and Environment Act 1987*. It details how a parcel of land is to be utilised and/or developed.

Subdivision of land

Paperwork for the land subdivision will be finalised and submitted to authorities by the land surveyor. Each state has their own requirements for documentation, so you'll need to refer to the local land registry to understand what is needed. These certificates and documents will also form part of the contract documentation for the sales.

Building surveyor

Your quantity surveyor (QS) and building surveyor will confirm all works are complete. This is a requirement for the bank, and it is only once this has been done that they will issue final payments to the builder, less retention. Remember that the retention is the amount you withhold from the builder for potential defects during the defects liability period (DLP).

Finance

As mentioned, final payments to the builder will be made. The lender will also begin preparations for settlements for sales proceeds to be received.

Inspections

Buyers who purchased off the plan will be advised that inspections of their completed dwellings can take place. The sales agent/s can also commence their marketing and selling for any residual stock. We'll cover this in more detail shortly.

Consultants

Verify with all consultants such as architects or building designers, town planners, engineers, builders, agents, solicitors and surveyors that all of your agreed works have been completed and nothing is outstanding.

Sales and marketing

Understanding how to market and ultimately sell your completed development is extremely important and can determine how successful your project will be in terms of profit. You'll need to choose the right sales agent who knows the market and has a good database of potential investors or owner-occupiers. Questions you'll need to consider include: do you market for sales off-the-plan; do you show potential buyers through 'off-market' as construction nears completion; or do you go to auction?

Residential

The way you present the property on completion when it comes to furnishing for marketing photos will play a huge role in the success of your development. Do you stage the property more towards downsizers, or do you stage it so that the property presents as more child-friendly? Can you use space creatively, such as by adding a study nook or desk area?

Artificial intelligence (AI) is now playing a big part in how properties are presented online. A lot of the styling and furnishing you see for online listings is 'photoshopped'. More sophisticated buyers or those looking at higher-end products will pay attention to this, as they want to feel that the product they're buying is premium. Investors will have less emotion, so using AI won't have a huge impact on potential sale prices with them.

There are so many options to consider, but having the right team around you will help you to determine the best way to go. Understanding your target market will also help define how you advertise and market the property.

Commercial

When it comes to commercial property, particularly industrial, your marketing will focus on the functionality of the property:

- How high is the truss clearance?
- How many roller doors are there and what height are they?
- Is the complex or property secure with security fencing and/or cameras?
- What is the gross floor area (GFA)?
- How big is the office space?
- What amenities are provided?
- How much power is available?
- How much parking is available?
- Is there a mezzanine? If so, is it timber, steel or concrete construction?
- What is the mezzanine load rating?

The list goes on!

Often the sales agent who presented you with the site will want the eventual listing when you complete the development, but be careful! Ensure that the agent you choose has experience and previous success in selling a similar product. Some agents are fantastic at selling development sites but not necessarily the best at selling completed product.

Fees

Agents' commissions are a big cost to consider. This cost will come out of the settlement fees. Agents will generally charge a commission on the sale of anywhere between 1.5 per cent and 3 per cent depending on the type and value of the property.

Opting for a cheaper fee might result in a lower sale price, thus reducing your profit. The time it takes for your development to sell is also important. This stage of the project is when your interest costs will be the highest, especially if you need to apply for an extension, so selling quickly for the best possible price ensures you can pay all outstanding debts, receive the money you personally invested into the project and then finally receive your profit!

The settlement process

Now that you have your agreed sale prices, it's time to prepare for settlement. This is where your solicitor or conveyancer comes back into the picture. They will have pre-drafted contracts to provide to the buyers, but you'll need to consider with each offer what their terms are.

Are they unconditional offers or do they require further inspections, due diligence or finance clauses? As a seller, an unconditional offer is the best you can receive. You'll also want to consider settlement timeframes, along with the deposit amount.

Issuing of titles

As mentioned, there is a lot of documentation that needs to be completed for a sale to go through. One of the most important is the issuing of titles. We've seen many circumstances where the titles office has caused delays due to information such as survey plans not being accurate or missing information. As a result, the settlements can push out, and buyers may, in the worse case scenario, be able to terminate the contract. This will leave you empty-handed – not the desired result when you're so close to the end!

The same goes for any building defects and obtaining sign-off from authorities, such as council, water boards and power providers. These delays can impact your profit margin substantially. Accurate documentation and understanding exactly what each party requires to sign off on the project is critical.

Fingers crossed this book has helped you understand what will be required along the way so that when you reach settlement, it's smooth and painless. With each passing settlement, funds will be distributed as per your agreements to lenders, financiers or investor partners. Generally, all outstanding debts are paid out first and government taxes such as GST come next. You'll then be reimbursed for any money you put into the project, and finally, you'll receive your profit!

Once you've completed your development, all the relevant paperwork has been stamped and everything is ticked off, you've done it! You've achieved what many dream of but few ever manage. You're ready now to learn what to do once you've hit completion: buy, sell or hold, and your exit-strategy options. To understand more about what comes next, read on.

PART VI
POST-DEVELOPMENT, NOW WHAT?

With construction completed, you're almost at the finish line! You can stand back, admire what you've built and enjoy the satisfaction of knowing that you and your team have worked hard to get to this point. Creating a home for a person or a location for a new business is a wonderful way to add value to society and people's lives. Do it well and you'll leave an indelible mark on communities that lasts well into the future.

In Part VI we share with you some tips to survive market downturns, plus what we see on the horizon for the future of property development – and how this can affect you.

CHAPTER SIXTEEN
WHAT ARE YOUR OPTIONS?

Once you've achieved practical completion, you'll need to make some decisions about what to do next. It's a good time to think like a poker player: to know when to hold 'em and when to fold 'em.

Understanding what the right move is and when to make it will pay off – hopefully – and you can look forward to reaping the benefits according to your strategy. Ideally, your next move should fulfil your feasibility from the start of your development, which will be different for every developer depending on their objectives, portfolio and personal situation. Your strategy can change too as your circumstances change, but your trusted team will always be on hand to guide you towards the best options.

This chapter outlines the two options with developments.

Sell

Selling a property is a tough decision. Ideally, you want to hold on to your properties long term as they deliver you an income. So, before you consider selling, run the numbers carefully and calculate your return on the property, taking into account stamp duty, purchasing costs, selling costs and capital gains tax (CGT).

Remember, if you're planning to sell the property and replace it with another, you'll need to pay stamp duty and purchasing costs again, which can add up to more than 10 per cent of the cost of the property just to swap one property for another.

Here are the main options for how to sell your development:

- Sell before any work is done. In this scenario, you get offered a much higher price from another developer even if you have not done work on the development yet. We've had situations like this before, including a client who bought a 200-acre site in Mittagong, New South Wales, in the early 2010s for $2 million, only to be offered $3 million for it even before the property settled!
- Sell with the DA in place but no turning of soil yet.
- Sell part of the completed project (and retain some for future wealth).
- Sell the entire completed project.

You might also choose to sell:

- when it's a sellers' market – that is, there are lots of buyers in the market and you can achieve a top price
- if the market looks to be heading into a downturn – it may be worth selling before the herd is aware (we cover this in the next chapter)
- when interest rates are rising and you believe the market might go flat or turn
- if part of your portfolio review process reveals a property that is underperforming and, based on your research and assumptions, will continue to underperform in the future.

If you're considering selling because the value of the property has grown significantly and you need funds to invest in a better project, ask yourself the following questions:

- How does selling fit into my plan?
- Where will I put the profits?
- How leveraged is my portfolio?
- What's my risk profile?
- What's my exit strategy?

Hold

There are a few reasons why investors don't sell their properties. Property is a top-performing asset class, and over the long term the median house price continues to trend upwards. You can also leverage one property to buy another, and your tenants are effectively paying your mortgages indefinitely. Also, if you sell, you pay tax on 50 per cent of the property's capital gains (its increase in value); instead, you could refinance the equity into another property or redraw equity. Holding property and never selling means you'll never pay CGT; essentially, this means that when you refinance you can use profit that isn't taxed.

Generally, the long-term history of property shows that selling is a bad idea unless you're moving that money to a higher-quality asset or better opportunity.

The main options to hold your development include the following:

- Hold the property in the short term, if you're in a buyers' market and can afford to hold the property, to wait for it to turn to a sellers' market when the market has picked up.
- Hold the property in the long term to get multiple cycles of capital growth and build a passive income.

You might also choose to hold if the area the property is in is gentrifying and has growth prospects, or if interest rates are dropping.

Don't sell a property just because you don't 'like' it – property investing is about the numbers! We find so many people sell properties because they continually have minor maintenance issues. The few thousand dollars a year they pay may seem like a huge headache, but if the property is growing in value by tens of thousands of dollars per year it's still a great investment!

If there is equity in the property, either from your development margin or from capital growth during the project, you may be able to refinance with a lender. Normally, this would be a first- to third-tier standard loan to pull out the equity and fund another investment or development. This is typically done when looking to hold the property but extract as much equity to either buy another investment property or put as many funds as possible into the next development project.

Exit strategies

When you're investing in property of any kind, you need to have an exit strategy; choosing one should be part of your preparatory planning. Your exit strategy will be different depending on your goals, portfolio and personal circumstances – a financial planner may be helpful here to provide advice on what could be most appropriate for you. Your strategy may also change as your circumstances evolve, but it can guide your decisions along the way.

Some investors will transition to higher-cash-flow properties, such as commercial property, to build a larger passive income. If you're interested in commercial property, please refer to Steve's book *Commercial Property Investing Explained Simply*, and if you wish to read about portfolio planning strategies in the long term, refer to *Residential Property Investing Explained Simply*.

As a basic refresher, here are the six most common exit strategies you could use when looking to capitalise on your property investments:

1. Keep all your properties and don't pay down your debt.
2. Keep all your properties but pay down your debt.
3. Keep all your properties and increase your debt.
4. Sell part of your portfolio to pay down your debt.
5. Sell part of your portfolio and live off the profit.
6. Sell your whole portfolio.

CHAPTER SEVENTEEN
SURVIVING MARKET DOWNTURNS

You might think you've hit the jackpot with your new development only to discover things take a turn for the worse, and suddenly the market hits a downturn. The most common types of downturns include:

- recessions
- pandemics
- change of legislation
- supply chain issues
- inflation, and costs of materials or labour going up
- rising interest rates
- location growth outside CBDs
- wars.

You might look at this list and think you've probably lived through all of these, and the fact is that big global change brings big global unrest and uncertainty. It's helpful to understand *why* downturns happen so that you can try to pick the market better, but it's also good to know that there's no real 'good' or 'bad' time to develop – everyone benefits from everything in some way, and you could do the same to create a great opportunity.

The good news is that for all of us the hardest times necessitate change. We need change to make way for prosperity again and the chance to look for new opportunities as innovative and clever developers.

The best developers create strategies to future-proof their success. They adapt to the market with tactics to help them when the going gets tough, because they know that those who endure economic hardship often emerge on the other side stronger and more confident.

Here are the three top ways to protect yourself and your development when times get tough:

1. **Market analysis.** Do your research to consider all the market machinations. What are the population and demographic shifts? What is the balance between demand and supply? What is the government doing about it?

2. **Case studies.** Research what other countries have done in similar situations. Obviously, every market is unique, but it's helpful to understand how other developers have adapted to various conditions and what's worked for them.

3. **Strategic planning.** While it should inform your due diligence anyway, strategic thinking can help you consider from the beginning how you might plan for a downturn. If it happens, you'll be well placed to fill the gaps because you've already accounted for them.

What happens when you need to act immediately? The bottom has dropped out of the market and you need to create some swift changes. The best place to start is around your budget and what you can control. Here are our top ways to weather an incoming market storm:

- **Look carefully at your overheads.** Get rid of any non-essential expenses so that you can track your outgoings. Redistribute your budget towards anything that increases sales and profits. You could also look at renegotiating contractor and supplier prices.

- **Do a full audit.** Go through your feasibility report and look for ways to free up capital. If you've already looked at expenses and expenditure, you might consider your team. In tough times, your team will be a huge asset to you and your business and overall morale, but if you can down-staff somehow, it might be worthwhile to give you some breathing room.

- **Stress-test the project.** See how long you can survive this negative outcome, as it could mean you need to sell to minimise losses before it's too late.

CHAPTER EIGHTEEN
THE FUTURE OF DEVELOPMENT

No-one can predict the future, but we can use as much data as possible to make educated decisions. As former engineers and number nerds, we love data because data never lies! As we mentioned before, property development is a numbers game, and to crystal-ball your way into the future it's the hard numbers that will steer you in the right direction.

Typically, long-term data is the most important to consider, especially for holding a property. Yes, you must be mindful over the short term, but your asset will be worth more the longer you hold it. Property development is slightly different, though, because the short-term data (up to five years) is the most important, as this is the peak time to make your profit.

When it comes to the future of the housing market in Australia, there are things that we know and many that we don't. Here are some of the unknowns to be aware of:

- New taxes
- The future of interest rates
- Housing policies
- Election promises

- Superannuation changes
- Airbnb legislation
- The economy.

Specifically, here are some of the known things when it comes to the future of the housing market in Australia.

The housing market

The Australian housing market is often characterised nowadays as undersupplied. Supply is at the centre of government policy approaches to housing, and the latest reporting from Housing Australia estimates a supply shortfall of over 100,000 dwellings to the end of 2028.

Governments are very focused on housing. In November 2023, the Australian Government established the $10 billion Housing Australia Future Fund (HAFF) to 'provide additional funding to support and increase social and affordable housing, as well as other acute housing needs including, but not limited to, the particular needs of Indigenous communities and housing services for women, children and veterans.' Its core purpose is to invest for the benefit of future generations of Australians.

As a property developer, the opportunities for growth within these housing sectors will continue and we don't anticipate this slowing down.

Urban sprawl and regional migration

Despite climate concerns, Australians still prefer living near the coast and bushland, though affordability may challenge this trend. COVID-19 quickly increased the demand for satellite towns due to working from home and flexible working.

Focusing on these lifestyle locations with great fundamentals could be a great option when looking for your next development location. Keep in mind, though, that the pandemic-driven migration to regional areas is slowing, with some residents returning to capital cities for better connectivity and amenities.

Millennials

Love them or be confused by them, millennials represent the future of Australia. Millennials are now the largest adult cohort in Australia, and as a long-term property investor, you'll most likely be developing for this cohort and their needs, because they're increasingly entering the property market as first-time homebuyers.

This generational shift may boost demand for established homes, especially in specific urban areas. However, you have also probably seen news about how millennials struggle to get a foot on the property ladder, particularly in urban areas, where there is not only a huge undersupply but also there are affordability issues. However, this doesn't mean avoiding this demographic, as there are opportunities to gain extra profit margin with smart architectural and fit-out options.

Foreign investors

Demand from overseas buyers for Australian real estate during the second half of 2023 was double the level of the second half of 2019. This is likely to continue growing over the coming years.

Foreign investors are generally required to purchase new properties in Australia if they don't hold residency, within rules set by the Foreign Investment Review Board (FIRB). These rules are designed to increase the supply of new housing and protect existing housing stock for Australian residents. As a developer, this means you can build attractive stock for foreign investors, but they must receive FIRB approval.

Here's what you need to know:

- Foreign investors can buy newly constructed properties (referred to as '**new dwellings**') without restrictions, provided they comply with the FIRB. A new dwelling is typically a property that has not been previously occupied or sold.

- Foreign investors can buy **vacant land** but must commit to developing it by building a new dwelling within a specified timeframe (usually four years).
- **Non-residents** are generally are not permitted to purchase established (second-hand) residential properties unless under specific circumstances, such as redevelopment where the dwelling is demolished and new dwellings are constructed.
- **Temporary residents** can buy one established dwelling to live in, but they must sell it if they leave Australia.

Depending on your development location, you may style the type and fit-out of the property to suit certain foreign investors to be able to sell for a higher price.

Home ownership

Younger buyers are likely to enter the property market later and may start with smaller properties or apartments before upgrading to family homes. This should be a key consideration for the types of property development you undertake. Furthermore, some may continue renting while investing in property as an asset rather than as a primary residence. This may cause a shift to people building properties for renters over owner-occupiers, such as small town-houses or apartments in a typical owner-occupier area where buyers are priced out but still want to live.

As a result of these factors, we are seeing new ownership models hit the market. Creative ownership models, such as fractional ownership and shared equity, may become more prevalent as younger buyers seek alternative ways to enter the property market. Future business models might include property derivatives or publicly traded property portfolios.

The rise of renters

For those priced out of home ownership, lifelong renting may become more common, prompting changes in housing policy and an increase in build-to-rent (BTR) developments. We believe that future rental markets might offer additional services, such as bulk utilities, to attract and retain tenants. This is certainly an area to watch, and it's already a strong asset class in the UK where there are many BTR buildings. Closer to home, we are seeing BTR projects pop up in Melbourne and Sydney, and it will be interesting to see how developers further harness this market. We believe it will have an impact on smaller developments, with a changed approach to affordability in the area being developed.

High-density living

We've seen a few trends when it comes to pressures on urban population growth and affordability issues. One of these is the trend towards smaller lot sizes and more apartment living. You might also see this referred to as 'vertical living'. Despite shrinking lot sizes, house sizes remain relatively stable, indicating a shift in preferences toward maximising indoor space.

This is also why you're more likely to see subdivided blocks where two townhouses replace one house on the same block, with the same indoor space but half the yard. Mixed-use developments are another trend, where you can be creative with the way the site is used.

Technology

As technology develops at a rapid rate, we believe we'll see more 'smart houses' in the future. This is not related to sustainability but more to technology and renter and owner experiences. Think about 20 years ago when we didn't have smartphones. Nowadays, homes use cloud-based voice systems such as Alexa and Google to do everything from play music to check security alarm systems while the occupier is overseas. In the next 20 years, the internals and externals of our houses may have completely different technological requirements.

Sustainability

Growing environmental concerns and government incentives are likely to drive demand for energy-efficient homes.

When it comes to the future of property development, there are a lot of great reasons to do sustainable projects. They're better for the environment, last longer, are healthier to live in and, in terms of feasibility, can command a higher price and value, which makes them good investments.

Sustainable developments are projects that have a stronger focus on using environmentally better products, materials, building techniques and processes. They consider the whole life cycle of the development, including design, construction, use and end-of-life, with benefits including reducing material waste, reducing operating and use costs, and better thermal comfort, health and wellbeing.

In Australia, new homes must comply with certain minimum standards and building requirements. While they're technically voluntary, they're often part of legislation that makes them a must for building and the industry as a whole. These minimum standards include the Green Star rating system, GreenSmart®, BASIX and NatHERS, which each assess consumer products, services, the environment, construction, energy and water utilities. For example, today new homes must be built with a 7-star energy efficiency rating according to the Housing Industry Association (HIA), reflecting the huge focus on reducing energy costs and usage.

For developers, sustainable house design is a major movement only set to gather steam. More consumers are demanding their homes perform better than ever before, and there are huge opportunities to build greener, healthier and cheaper developments to benefit everyone. Homes with better energy ratings and systems could command a premium, while those that lag in sustainability may lose value. This is especially important if legislation changes and developments require updates.

Sustainable housing myths

Sustainable housing has come a long way since the days of 3-star energy ratings for new builds and solar panels on the roof, but there are still some pervasive myths in the marketplace:

1. **It's more expensive.** There is a pervasive myth in the industry that sustainable development is hugely expensive. Experts say that building a sustainable house is typically 5 to 8 per cent more expensive than a more traditional house, but this is offset by the future built-in savings through construction materials and techniques for power, water, thermal energy and solar.

2. **It requires specialist products.** Where once the choices to build sustainable developments were limited, there is now greater awareness in the marketplace and more options bringing down costs overall. There are builders all over Australia who are well-versed in sustainable design and construction, and some are simply using products already available on the market, rather than turning to specialist materials to achieve it.

3. **It looks ugly.** We are seeing the opposite – well-designed homes that hold their value and have better potential for stronger resale. You only need to look at the highest-end suburbs in our cities, where many sustainable house designs are showcased almost as a badge of honour, making them super stylish. We know that whoever lives there is not going to be forking over a lot of money for energy, and we also know that these developments will only continue to improve design-wise with the underlying driver that they're better by all accounts. In this landscape of cost-of-living pressures, that's a good news story.

Passive housing

The 'passive house' is the next evolution of sustainable housing. It's a rigorous building energy performance standard that aims to reduce buildings' energy use and maximise occupant comfort and health. Already big in places like Melbourne and Tasmania, there are many good-quality builders applying the passive house methodologies.

Think of it like building a completely airtight home where there are virtually no defects and the risk of water damage is eliminated altogether (water damage being the enemy of house construction). By adhering to passive house standards, homes enjoy the benefits of improved energy efficiency and good insulation, and because they require so little to operate, occupiers save money on heating and cooling to live comfortably year-round. The standard follows five principles:

1. Continuous insulation
2. High-performance windows
3. An airtight building envelope
4. Heat recovery ventilation
5. Thermal bridge–free construction.

A passive house is also better for the environment, with excellent sustainability properties – namely, generating fewer greenhouse gas emissions and having a lower carbon footprint.

While the passive house methodology is not widely adopted, we believe that variations of the theme are coming. In the same way that solar panels have been adopted as part and parcel of the construction process, along with the government's support of energy agendas, we expect models that promote sustainability will continue to grow and become more mainstream. It's only a matter of time.

Furthermore, just because (most) developers won't be living in their developments doesn't mean that sustainable housing won't take off. As long as the demand is there from the consumer – the investor – they will find their place in the development landscape.

Developers will continue to see innovations in this space. For some developers, it's enough that sustainable housing aligns with their ethical and philosophical values, but most will need to see a return on investment that makes putting in the time and money worthwhile.

Our takeaways

Here are our main considerations when it comes to the future of property development in Australia:

- Millennial preferences will significantly shape the Australian property market over the next decade.
- Lifestyle regions outside of the major capital cities, especially on the fringes of capital cities, will have increased demand, offering excellent opportunities.
- Home ownership paths may become longer, with younger buyers exploring new ownership models.
- Renters will gain more influence in the housing market, potentially leading to new policies and rental-focused developments.
- High-density living will increase, with backyards becoming rarer.
- It will be advantageous to develop properties with as much technological innovation or ability to be retrofitted as easily as possible.
- Energy efficiency and climate risk will increasingly influence property values.

PART VII
CASE STUDIES

Whether you opt for traditional building or want to shoot for the stars and try something more radical, remember that developing is a numbers-driven game. But with so much data, spreadsheets and feasibilities, it can be tricky to see how a development comes to life without context and the story behind the digits. Let us introduce you to four case studies so you can learn what to do right – and what can go very wrong!

Over decades of collective experience, we've worked with hundreds of consultants and property professionals. Their stories are wild! With many things in life, you have to jump in and learn along the way, but when you're developing property the stakes are so much higher – personally, financially and professionally. These four case studies illustrate how making the wrong decisions can impact a development. We've chosen different types of properties (all by real-life developers – our clients and peers), along with timelines and feasibility tables, so you can see how no-one is immune to the importance of setting your BIGFIGs and doing your due diligence from the start.

CHAPTER NINETEEN

DEALING WITH SQUATTERS IN A TOWNHOUSE DEVELOPMENT

Brett completed a three-townhouse development in Berwick, an outer suburb of Melbourne. He paid for the site in cash, but it didn't go completely to plan. His biggest problem was dealing with squatters, who took over. Luckily, by paying cash he absorbed a lot of the issues and delays.

How it started

Brett did this development as a long-term 'buy and hold' strategy. He wanted a property to potentially downsize his parents into and achieve further capital growth. He bought in the old part of Berwick with the knowledge that there were some planning changes being proposed that would prevent future townhouse/unit developments in that area, which has a high demand from downsizers and first home buyers. It also provided a solution for him personally with his own family. A lot of the project was self-funded – he used money from his business and available redraw from other properties to fund it.

One of the townhouses was sold to a lady who approached the builder when they were about three-quarters finished asking if the townhouses were going to be for sale. She had sold her farm to a developer for big bucks and was looking to downsize. She paid $1 million for one, which was about $50k over what Brett was originally happy to sell them for.

What went wrong?

Before the old house was to be demolished, a group of squatters took up residence in it and made it extremely difficult to progress with the development, even though Brett had his permits. In the end, he experienced a 12-month delay because he had to go to the Victorian Civil and Administrative Council (VCAT) three times to try and get the squatters removed. In his experience, VCAT was highly ineffective, which pushed out the delays. The squatters were finally moved on, and he was able to demolish the house one week later and push on with the development.

The fun didn't stop there, though. When clearing the old house, the demolishers damaged the brick wall of the neighbour's garage. This had to be repaired as part of the building works, and work on the development couldn't commence until the issue was fixed.

Then, the planning scheme overlays were altered mid-project. This meant that the subdivision and title process couldn't go through until after the occupancy permits were issued at the end, instead of when they were at lock-up stage. This meant another delay, this time for four months.

Finally, Brett copped an extra-high private open space contributions fee from the council due to the part of the municipality in which the development was located.

Townhouse development timeline

Date	Event
August 2017	Settled on property
April 2018	Planning permit / development approval issued (quicker than anticipated)
Late 2018	The start of construction was anticipated, but squatters took over
2018-2019	Three trips to VCAT to try and remove the squatters
September 2019	Old house demolished (one week after squatters vacated)
November 2019	Neighbouring garage wall repaired before construction could commence
December 2019	Construction commenced - slabs down before Christmas
October 2020	Construction completed - the builder didn't muck around!
April 2021	Individual titles were finally through, and the new purchasers were in via leaseback

How it ended up

Cash flow–wise, this wasn't the best investment, but because Brett used cash for the land purchase, it didn't cost him anything to hold. Furthermore, he could have built two larger homes and made a better profit than he made on building three townhouses due to the open space contributions. You live and learn!

However, the biggest advantage the development afforded him was that he can hold it to use personally in the future if he needs to, or he can cash out of it for a larger profit. Because much of the project was self-funded and he claimed interest costs against other properties, this lowered the risk when it came to holding costs, and the overall interest on the development was quite low too. As a result, the profit margin he achieved was still above 31 per cent (or more than $700k) despite all of the challenges. This is very hard to achieve for a townhouse project in today's market; anything close to 20 per cent profit is a great result now, with build costs increasing substantially along with land values.

Townhouse feasibility

Property acquisition	
Property price	$790,000
Transaction costs	$48,137
Development and building permits	$25,000
Finance	
Finance costs	$3,100
Interest	$58,000
Construction	
Demolition of existing building	$22,000
Construction costs (building contracts)	$1,128,435
Construction contingency	$23,000
Holding costs	$19,000
Rental revenue (12-month lease of original dwelling following acquisition)	$20,800
Titles	$85,000
Marketing	
Agents commission	$17,460
Selling costs	$3,950
Total development cost	$2,202,282
Total development revenue	$2,920,000
Total development profit	**$717,718**

CHAPTER TWENTY
DEALING WITH DELAYS IN A DUPLEX DEVELOPMENT

Adrian is a developer based in New South Wales. He began a development in 2023 on a site in Thirroul, a northern seaside suburb in the city of Wollongong, south of Sydney. Adrian planned to develop a duplex – in this case, two double-storey townhouses side by side – which became thwarted by delays.

How it started

Adrian planned to do a duplex with an investment partner under a 'develop and sell' strategy for profit. Duplexes are very popular types of developments, especially for first-time developers, and although Adrian isn't a first-timer – he's been working in the industry for many years – the lengthy delays throughout the process almost resulted in him giving up the game altogether.

His key objective was to respond to a niche in the market. He wanted to create a high-end project with a low-maintenance lifestyle. He believed this would appeal to both downsizers and high-net-worth families who were either local or moving into the area from Sydney with the attraction of getting more bang for their buck.

What went wrong?

The delays were the most problematic aspect of the entire process. All of these delays were out of Adrian's control and caused considerable cost and time issues.

First, his electricity company did not make the request for the abolishment or notify him (until he called them asking for an update) that the landowners needed to countersign it. This added four weeks to the program.

There was also a significant delay due to cadastral (land parcel boundary) realignment. As he began demolishing the existing dwelling and marking out the slab location, he realised that the edge of the slab on the western edge was within 900mm of the neighbour's retaining wall (which he thought was also the boundary). Adrian's surveyor investigated and found that the cadastral boundary survey for the whole northern side of the road was out of alignment by 380mm. To rectify this, the surveyor needed to re-survey every single dwelling on the northern side of the road and then resubmit a cadastral boundary survey for the street to NSW Land Registry Services for approval. This added another five weeks to the program.

Finally, the weather. This one's tricky because you can never plan for clear days, but Adrian experienced inclement weather at the worst time. When it came time to pour the slab, he had wet weather every day. This meant that it took a further three weeks to get the slab down. All up, there were around three months of delays, which added significant cost because they impacted other deadlines and timelines.

Duplex development timeline

Date	Milestone
August 2023	Site acquisition
January 2024	CDC approval
March 2024	Service disconnections
April 2024	Demolition
May 2024	Construction commencement
March 2025	Target construction completion following the delays

How it ended up

All of the issues were worth it because the views at the development's location are amazing. The site provides ocean views to the south and east, and clear escarpment views to the rear. This is a rare and highly desirable combination for future owners, so Adrian knew it was worth pushing through the pain because he would end up with a highly appealing development that would sell easily.

Despite the issues that arose, which were out of his control and hard at the time, he always had his eye on the bigger picture: developing with an investment partner to create profits for both parties to financially benefit.

Duplex feasibility

Property acquisition	
Acquisition price	$1,930,000
Transaction costs	$102,060
Development and building permits	$73,537
Finance	
Finance costs	$0
Interest	$311,472
Construction	
Demolition of existing building	$35,000
Construction costs (building contracts)	$1,577,250
Construction contingency	$38,694
Holding costs	$6,900
Rental revenue (six-month lease of original dwelling following acquisition)	$21,000
Titles	$26,705
Marketing	
Agents commission	$82,450
Selling costs	$17,400
Total development cost (incl. GST)	$4,180,468
Claim on GST input credit	$167,897
Total development cost (excl. GST)	$4,012,571
Total development revenue (incl. GST)	$4,871,000
Remittance of GST	$267,364
Total development revenue (excl. GST)	$4,603,636
Total development profit	**$591,065**

CHAPTER TWENTY-ONE

DEALING WITH FUNDING IN A VILLA COMPLEX

Jacinta is a project manager who thought she'd try her luck creating an affordable apartment product in northwest Tasmania. She built a complex of ten villas comprising one- and two-bedroom villas. Despite some lengthy delays, all were bought by single women and single mothers.

How it started

Jacinta made a strategic decision to create a product with an affordable price tag, applying the 'JV with a landowner' strategy. The ten villas included eight two-bedroom, one-bathroom, one-car-garage configurations (priced at $450,000) and two one-bedroom, one-bathroom, one-car-garage configurations (priced at $385,000). Interestingly, all ten were bought by single women and single mothers, with a mix of interstate and local buyers. The price point and dwellings were a good fit for the buyers and this market.

What went wrong?

Jacinta had limited funds for a development project ($430,000 with no serviceability). The project was for sale with a DA in place, and while it had some decent profit, she didn't have enough cash to complete it.

As the complex took two years from initial feasibility to completion, Jacinta was keen to ensure the villas sold quickly. However, because the development was in a small town of about 6000 people, the sales took 12 months longer than expected. This meant she needed to extend finance by six months, which was costly. She thought she would gain pre-sales while the villas were under construction, but people in Tasmania like to see the finished product before committing, so this caused further delays.

Also, the valuation came in lower than expected for the construction loan finance, so she needed to find extra funds to cover the shortfall.

Finally, the onsite stormwater detention was an issue as the site fell away from the street. The council decided at the last moment that they wanted an additional tank under the driveway, which had to be sourced quickly. In a large rain event, the pump kept getting overheated, so she needed to add another pump to the system.

To help, the landowner agreed to stay in the deal, which meant she didn't have to pay the full cost of the land upfront. Jacinta paid out her loan on the land, transferred the land to a unit trust so all parties were on title, and then used the remainder of the cash to complete the deal. Each party – the landowner, project manager and JV money partners – took a percentage profit share at the end.

Villa development timeline

Date	Milestone
April 2021	JV with landowner agreement
October 2021	Development approval
February 2022	Construction commencement
April 2023	Construction completion
April 2023	Initial targeted sales completion
April 2024	Final sales completed

How it ended up

The most rewarding aspect of this process was providing housing for single women and creating a space that could grow into a community. Although Jacinta lost some profit due to the high lending costs and the length of the project, there was still some good profit for all parties. It required a creative solution to achieve a great result!

The development was also a learning opportunity about what the market wants. She was really surprised that the two one-bedders didn't get snapped up first. She thought that this product would have been sought after as it was priced more cheaply but had the same amount of living space (minus the extra bedroom). It seems that most people want the extra space for guests or storage, and she'll take that learning into the next development.

Villa complex feasibility

Property acquisition	
Acquisition price	$216,000
Transaction costs	$11,448

Development and building permits	$38,711
Finance	
Finance costs	$0
Interest	$236,000
Construction	
Demolition of existing building	$15,000
Construction costs (building contracts)	$2,501,187
Construction contingency	$116,134
Holding costs	$15,400
Rental revenue	$0
Titles	$26,705
Marketing	
Agents commission	$87,520
Selling costs	$26,256
Total development cost (incl. GST)	$3,290,361
Claim on GST input credit	$178,437
Total development cost (excl. GST)	$3,111,924
Total development revenue (incl. GST)	$4,376,000
Remittance of GST	$437,600
Total development revenue (excl. GST)	$3,938,400
Total development profit	**$826,476**

CHAPTER TWENTY-TWO

DEALING WITH LGAs IN A COMMERCIAL MIXED-USE DEVELOPMENT

Gerard was engaged by a developer on a design-and-construct basis to tackle a large development project on the south coast of New South Wales. Without needing to secure the site but simply build and project-manage it, it might have been straightforward, but problems were evident from the start.

How it started

Gerard was engaged by the developer for two multi-storey, mixed-use buildings on adjoining lots. Building 1 was three storeys of commercial space plus a fourth level with three residential apartments. Building 2 was originally designed to have the same specs but with a secure basement car park.

The development met high demand in the area, where many of the commercial spaces were old and dated. There was also demand for apartments in the area, particularly from government departments. By creating both, the buildings provided high-quality, modern commercial space.

What went wrong?

The first delay causing significant cost implications was that the local government area (LGA) planners failed to process the DA promptly and professionally. It took threats from the Land and Environment Court and intervention by councillors to force the planners to process the application. This pushed the construction into a new scope of the *National Construction Code 2019*, the building code that sets the standards for construction in Australia, resulting in the requirement for a sprinkler system to Building 1 that would not have been required under the *National Construction Code 2016*, which meant an additional cost to the development of about $250,000.

The second major delay caused by the LGA was related to a miscalculation of contributions and car spacings for Building 2. Gerard was only able to obtain a partial construction certificate until the issues were resolved. This process took more than 12 months and pushed the project into the purview of the *Design and Building Practitioners Regulation 2021*. Before this regulation came into effect, he could have designed a mixed-use building with

Class 2 dwellings of Type A construction; after the regulation came into effect, only registered design practitioners could do so.

Even with an approved DA, the council insisted he could not receive a construction certificate for the balance of works without having a registered design practitioner sign off. This would have cost more than $150,000 and an additional six-month delay to the project. In the end, the developer made the commercial decision to modify the design and replace the three Class 2 apartments, which would have sold for $700,000 to $800,000 each, to commercial space instead. Without the Class 2 component, the building no longer fell under the *Design and Building Practitioners Regulation 2021*.

This lack of accountability from LGA staff caused two years of delays on the project and costs to the developer in the order of $500,000!

Commercial mixed-use development timeline

Date	Milestone
Pre-2017	Site 1 is family-owned by developer
2017	Site 2 is acquired from an extended family member of the developer
November 2018	DA submission
October 2019	DA consent (11 months later!)
February 2020	Full construction certificate for Building 1; part construction certificate for ground floor of Building 2 Construction commencement of both buildings
May 2021	Building 2 part construction certificate works complete
June 2022	Building 2 balance of works construction certificate
July 2023	Final occupation certificate Building 1
August 2024	Final occupation certificate Building 2

How it ended up

Despite the delays and unforeseen costs, Gerard delivered a quality, high-demand product for the developer. At the time of writing, all three commercial spaces and the apartments have been sold in Building 1, and Building 2 has a government department as a tenant occupying three commercial floors and the secure basement car park with an exclusive option to lease the fourth commercial floor for the next six months. It has still been a profitable and worthwhile project for the developer, who is very happy with the result.

The property development process - explained simply

Educate yourself		
Books	Podcasts	Online resources

Assess your situation		
Current portfolio	Current finances	Risk profile

Make a plan		
Goals	Milestones	Exit strategies

Build your foundation team		
Accountant Property lawyer	Mortgage broker Real estate agent	Solicitor/Conveyancer Buyer's agent

Conduct initial feasibility		
BIGFIG 1: What are you buying the site for?	BIGFIG 2: What will it cost to build the development?	BIGFIG 3: What will you sell it for?

Build your team		
Development manager Town planner Landscape architect Interior designer	Project manager Architect/building designer Arborist Certifier	Surveyor Engineers Quantity surveyor Builder

Choose a buying structure		
Individual JV with equity partner	Company JV with landowner	JV with money or loan partner

Property acquisition		
Detailed Due Diligence	Negotiate purchase	Set up for settlement

Obtain finance		
Type of finance	Type of lender	Type of loan

Execute the development		
Secure approvals	Commence build	Practical completion

Make your money!		

EPILOGUE

Having made it through the book, you now have all the elements you need to kickstart your development goals, or at least whet your appetite with what's possible. For the two of us, development enables us to have the lifestyle we desire – more time with our families and more time to do the things that spark a flame in us. For example, during the writing of this book, Steve enjoyed some family time in the UK and then in Sicily. He even caught the athletics at the Olympic Games Paris 2024!

As well as reading the full story on property development, you now have the **full picture** with all three Property Explained Simply books. With these, you can make the best investment decisions based on what you're trying to achieve and your timeframe, borrowing capacity, budget and risk profile. Even if you never tackle a development, understanding the elements of this book can help your buy-and-hold residential and commercial investing with knowledge in value-adding down the track or buying a property with possibilities.

It's worth remembering that while the risks are great, so are the rewards. You can see by the volume of information in this book that executing a development from the start is a massive achievement and a testament to your ability to create something of immense value from nothing, but you must have the financial stability to get on the development ladder without putting yourself, your family or your business at any great risk. With good due diligence and a great team by your side, you can show the world you can do it!

We all know extreme wealth is not the key to happiness, so make sure you enjoy the process along the way. And make sure you celebrate the wins!

As with Steve's previous two books, we'd like to finish with a quote. This one seems fitting:

> *Ever since I was a child I have had this instinctive*
> *urge for expansion and growth. To me, the function*
> *and duty of a quality human being is the sincere and*
> *honest development of one's potential.*
>
> – Bruce Lee

ABOUT THE AUTHORS

Steve Palise is founder of Palise Property, one of Australia's fastest growing Buyer's Agents, and known as one of Australia's leading industry experts. Having acquired an impressive property portfolio that allowed him to leave salaried employment in his early thirties, he's now passionate about helping others to achieve their goals and financial freedom through property.

Liam Carmody is General Manager of Palise Property. From his previous career in Civil Engineering, Liam understands that first and foremost the numbers need to make sense particularly when it comes to investing in and developing property. He has amassed an enviable property portfolio himself as well as assisted hundreds of clients to improve their financial security through investing in property.

Scan the QR code to find out more about Palise Property and the services they offer.

ACKNOWLEDGEMENTS

This is my third book in the Property Explained Simply series, this one co-authored with Liam Carmody, whose first book it is. I think Liam now appreciates that writing and publishing a book takes teamwork. We would both therefore like to thank Annie Reid from Atrium Media, Lesley Williams and Will Allen from my publishers Major Street Publishing and our awesome cover designer Tess McCabe. Of course, I would not have been able to write my books without the support of my amazing team at Palise Property.

My mother passed away a year before this book was written. Ironically, she had no interest in property, but she instilled in me the importance of looking after the people around me. She believed this was the most important thing in life, and it's advice that I always try to follow.

Finally, I'd like to thank Lisa, my partner and mother of our beautiful little girl Rhea, for all the adventures we have been on together and plan to embark on in the future. Most of all, I'd like to thank her for the love and support she gives me every single day.

Steve

This book has been a long-term goal of mine and there's no way I could have achieved it without the support of some very important and special people. First, thank you Steve Palise for finally giving in and agreeing to complete the trilogy. Who would have thought a chance meeting in the UK a few years ago would have resulted in us writing a book together? It's amazing to watch the Palise Property business grow and I'm proud to be a part of it.

Thanks to Stan Waldren, for taking me under your wing back in 2005 and introducing me to property development. You continue to be an inspiration to me and I'm looking forward to continuing our relationship over the years ahead.

To my fellow professional colleagues Kylie Bazzi (World Class Conveyancing), Richie Muir (Lawlab), Jeremy Iannuzzelli (KHI Partners), Nick Wilcox (Blue Crane Capital) and David Dimovski (Davidbelle Design), your expertise and guidance is a huge reason this book contains the knowledge it does.

Thank you to those who feature in the case studies throughout this book: Adrian Cicino (Assured Developments), Gerard Turnbull (Construction & Design Australia), Jacinta van Lint and Brett, we appreciate you bravely sharing your stories.

Lastly, and certainly not least, the biggest thank you of all must go to my family. To my wife, Amie, there's no way I'd have done this without you. You are the reason I do what I do and we're now so privileged to watch our children grow up in our new home. We've already created so many amazing memories together and I can't wait to see what the future holds. To Killian, thanks for telling Daddy to stop building roads and to start building houses because there's more money in building houses. At four years old, you are already years ahead of me! To Orla, keep being the confident and funny little girl you are and bringing life and energy to our lives.

Liam

INDEX

rental income 6, 86
rental market 16
renters 193
reports 75-78
Residential Property Investing Explained Simply 184
residential development loans 127
residential developments 29-35
residential loan 134
residential property 131
residential sales 172-173
'resimercial' property 37
retail property 8, 37
retail finance 131
retention of payments 166
retirement 6, 38
retirement complex 63
return on investment (ROI) 13, 17
rising interest rates 182
risk 21, 33, 39, 141
risk and return 135
risk profiles 22-23, 96
rollover fees 112
rooming houses 42-43
RP Data 145

sale price 61, 65, 68, 129
self-managed superannuation funds (SMSFs) 15, 141
sellers' market 182
selling agents 41, 60, 64, 88
selling costs 48
selling property 127, 151
selling your development 88-89, 181-183
selling your property 185

senior debt 136, 137
sensitivity analysis 89-90, 145
setbacks 150
settlement 105, 106, 153-154
settlement agents 106
settlement process 174-175
sewer pump 84
sewerage rates 86
sign-offs 170-172, 175
site acquisition 72, 95
site management plans 161
site meetings 164, 168
site, finding the 55, 59-69
slab completion 166
small businesses 41
soil testing 162
soil types 146, 148
solicitors 93, 101
special needs housing 44
specialised commercial property 45
specialist disability accommodation (SDA) 44-45
specialty developments 42-48
split loans 113
squatters 204
stage selling 33, 35
stages of payments 166-167
staging for sale 78, 89, 173
stamp duty 12, 72, 143
strata costs 31, 34, 39
strata title 49, 86, 87
strategic planning 187
stress-testing 122, 188
structural engineers 77, 83
structures 24, 72, 119, 138
subdivision of land 171

OTHER BOOKS IN THE PROPERTY EXPLAINED SIMPLY SERIES

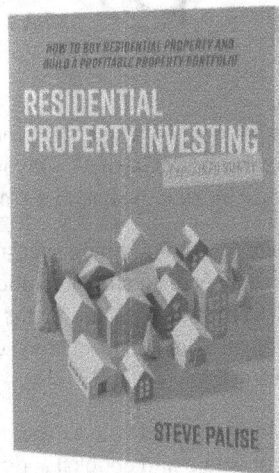

Published by and available from Major Street Publishing
and all good bookstores.

Ebooks also available from your favourite ebook supplier.

MAJOR
STREET

Be better with business books

MAJOR STREET

We hope you enjoy reading this book. We'd love you to post a review on social media or your favourite bookseller site. Please include the hashtag #majorstreetpublishing.

Major Street Publishing specialises in business, leadership, personal finance and motivational non-fiction books. If you'd like to receive regular updates about new Major Street books, email info@majorstreet.com.au and ask to be added to our mailing list.

Visit majorstreet.com.au to find out more about our books (print, audio and ebooks) and authors, read reviews and find links to our Your Next Read podcast.

We'd love you to follow us on social media.

in linkedin.com/company/major-street-publishing

f facebook.com/MajorStreetPublishing

instagram.com/majorstreetpublishing

X @MajorStreetPub